Revenue Recognition

Revenue Recognition

Principles and Practices

Frank J. Beil

First published in 2013 by
Business Expert Press, LLC
222 East 46th Street, New York, NY 10017
www.businessexpertpress.com

ISBN-13: 978-1-60649-594-0 (paperback)

ISBN-13: 978-1-60649-595-7 (e-book)

Business Expert Press Financial Accounting and Auditing Collection

Collection ISSN: 2151-2795 (print)
Collection ISSN: 2151-2817 (electronic)

Cover and interior design by Exeter Premedia Services Private Ltd., Chennai, India

First edition: 2013

10 9 8 7 6 5 4 3 2 1

Printed in the United States of America.

Abstract

Revenue is the "top" line on the income statement and is the fundamental driver of business success. It is essential that managers and executives understand the complexities involved in recognizing revenue under Generally Accepted Accounting Principles (GAAP) in the US Revenue Recognition principles are , are primarily concerned with two things: (a) the **timing aspect** (the when issue) and (b) the **amount to be recorded** (the how much issue). This book will provide extensive guidance in assisting managers with the appropriate answers to the two questions above for their companies.

This book is principally designed for managers and executives who have organizational responsibility for delivering results in the form of "profits" for their organizations. The book will be a comprehensive yet readable examination of the existing rules of revenue recognition for corporate entities. After reading the book, the manager or executive will have a thorough understanding of how accountants measure and record revenue. This "skill-set" will prove invaluable in understanding the impact that their business decisions will have on the financial statements with an emphasis on the income statement and the statement of cash flows.

The book will also have an executive-level overview of the proposed "IASB and FASB Standard: Revenue from Contracts with Customers."

Keywords

arrangements, fixed or determinable, stand-alone value, deliverables, variable consideration, performance obligations, rights of return, performance models, customer acceptance, allocation, multiple element arrangement, revenue recognition, completed performance, proportional performance, product revenue, service revenue, contracts with customers

Contents

Examples Index

CHAPTER 1

The Big Picture

Fundamental Concepts

About This Chapter

Revenue is the "top" line on the income statement and is the fundamental driver of business success. It is essential that managers and executives understand the complexities involved in recognizing revenue under Generally Accepted Accounting Principles (GAAP) as that the US Revenue Recognition is primarily concerned with two things; (1) the *timing aspect* (the when issue) and (2) *the amount to be recorded* (the how much issue).

This book is principally designed for managers and executives who have organizational responsibility for delivering results in the form of "profits" for their organizations. The book is a comprehensive yet readable examination of the existing rules of revenue recognition for corporate entities. After reading the book, the manager or executive will have a thorough understanding of how accountants measure and record revenue. This "skill-set" will prove invaluable in understanding the impact that their business decisions will have on the financial statements with an emphasis on the income statement and the statement of cash flows.

When reading through the book to develop a thorough understanding of how revenue arrangements and transactions impact your company's financial statements, please keep two things in mind. The first is that accounting for revenue arrangements requires the use of professional judgment in determining the "proper" accounting for your company in recording transactions that impact your financial statements. These decisions, regarding revenue recognition, will have an enormous impact on the financial health and performance of your company. Choose wisely. The second item is to consistently apply the professional judgments you have made in recording revenue to each reporting period. That is why it is vital that management personnel have a breadth and depth of understanding of how revenue arrangements are recorded and their impact on the company's financial statements. It is the purpose of this book.

The book will also have an executive-level overview of the proposed "IASB and FASB Standard: Revenue from Contracts with Customers" that will be released sometime in 2013.

General Guidance

Revenue recognition, as recorded in the financial statements, is the result of a sales transaction with a customer. In order for a company to record revenue, two conceptual criteria must be satisfied. The first criteria is that revenue to be recorded has to be *earned* and the second is that the consideration to be received has to be *realizable*.

1. Earned "revenues are considered to have been earned when the entity has substantially accomplished what it must do to be entitled to the benefits represented by the revenues."[1] These two concepts are the foundational principles of revenue recognition and have guided the Financial Accounting Standards Board (FASB) and the Securities and Exchange Commission (SEC) in their development of accounting principles and practices related to the recognition of revenue for companies.

When Is Revenue Earned?

Companies "earn" revenue from the delivery of goods, the performance of services, providing information, permitting buyers to use assets (leasing), providing others with access to intellectual property (licensing), or almost any other activity in which one party to the contract pays the other party for services and use of property. The activities performed by the seller to fulfill the promises made to the buyer are referred to in accounting as the "earnings process."

Revenue is recognized when the earnings process that relates to the promised deliverables (goods, services, right to use assets) is complete. Until the company completes the activities it has promised the buyer, revenue should not be recognized. In the case of cash payments made by the buyer to the seller prior to the seller fulfilling his or her promised activities, the seller should defer revenue recognition until he or she has delivered on the seller's obligations to the buyer. In accounting for revenue, the timing of cash payments and the earning of revenue are two separate and distinct accounting processes. They may, however, be linked in service contracts covering multiple periods. In this case, cash received on a systematic and regular basis for services rendered may indicate that the earnings process is complete for work performed for that time period.

In businesses whose primary business processes consist of delivering products to customers, the earnings process is generally straightforward. Revenue is generally recognized when the company delivers goods to the customer. However, in other revenue transactions, it may be more difficult in determining revenue recognition for activities being performed by the seller. For example:

Service Company, a management consulting firm, has been hired by Manufacturing Company to prepare an analysis and a report on "Improving Supply Chain Efficiencies." The report will be prepared over a six-month period with monthly reports to executives and a final report to be given as a presentation to management. Billings to Manufacturing Company occur as each monthly report is delivered.

An earnings analysis in this case would support two different conclusions.

1. The process is complete at the end of each month because seller can bill buyer, evidencing that the contract consists of six separate earnings processes.
2. The consulting firm concludes that the final report and presentation are the deliverables to the company and evidence completion of the earnings process.

In other transactions, the company may bundle goods and services together and charge one price for both the product and service deliverables. The revenue-recognition problem then is twofold:

1. When is the earnings process complete?
2. What amount of the consideration received needs to be allocated to the mix of goods and services?

These types of revenue transactions are referred to as multiple-element arrangements and will be the focus of Chapter 2: Multiple-Element Arrangements.

When Is Revenue Realizable?

Revenue is considered to be realizable when the seller has received consideration in the form or cash or claims to other assets from the buyer. The realization concept implies that the amount of consideration received (think cash or an account receivable) is an enforceable claim against the buyer and represents the amount of revenue to be recorded by the seller. Revenue is recognized when it is recorded in the records of the company. For revenue to be recognized, it first must be realized. In general, the recognition/realization of revenue occurs when the seller delivers on his or her promises and the buyer is obligated to transfer cash or other assets to the seller. Acceptance of products or services by the buyer creates an enforceable claim for the seller against the customer.

There are, however, sales arrangements that provide the seller with uncertainty as to "when" the realizability criterion is satisfied. For example, many companies sell goods with a specific right-of-return provision for the customer. In this instance, the question for revenue recognition becomes: Can we recognize revenue on delivery given the uncertainty of which customers will avail themselves of the option to return the products? Other revenue arrangements may include a clause that the customer may return the product or qualify for a refund unless the product or service meets customer specifications.

The presence of this contractual option may indicate that while payment is due on delivery, the seller warrants that the product will deliver value to the buyer by virtue of its integration with other equipment in pro products for third-party customers. In the case where the delivered equipment fails to be fully integrated with the company's other equipment, the customer is entitled to a 30% rebate of the purchase price. In this case, the seller would generally have to defer revenue recognition until the customer has accepted the product and the seller has met customer specifications.

Principles of Revenue Recognition

The development of revenue-recognition guidance built on the foundational concepts of earned and realizability was approached differently by the FASB and the SEC. The FASB's revenue-recognition guidance is transaction specific or industry specific. The SEC took the approach of providing more specific guidance that clarifies the concepts of earned and realizable.

The SEC Publication Topic 13, Revenue in Financial Statements,[2] specifies the four cornerstones that are required to be attained by the end of an accounting period (quarterly for public companies, annually for private companies) in order to record revenue from a revenue transaction. These four principles become accepted accounting practice for both public and private companies in complying with GAAP. The four criteria are:

1. Persuasive evidence of an arrangement
2. Delivery has occurred or services have been rendered
3. The seller's price to the buyer is fixed or determinable
4. Collectability is reasonably assured.

Persuasive Evidence

When performing an analysis of whether or not it is necessary to determine the obligations (deliverables) that the seller has promised to deliver, it is essential to refer to the contractual arrangement. Evidence of an arrangement allows the seller to analyze the obligations promised and to make a determination as to when he or she has fulfilled the seller's obligations to the customer. In addition, persuasive evidence provides the basis for enforceable claims that the customer is obligated to pay.

Persuasive evidence generally would require the seller to document the sales transaction in writing in a formal sales contract. However, this standard also allows arrangements that represent a company's normal business practices. For example, seller and buyer negotiate a master sales agreement that allows the buyer, at any time, to order product from the seller via use of Electronic Data Interchange (EDI). In this case, the seller can recognize revenue on delivery of products without a specific sales contract for the transaction.

The following illustrates the accounting issues involved in determining persuasive evidence of an arrangement.[3]

Fact Set

Company A has product available to ship to customers prior to the end of its current fiscal quarter. Customer B places an order for the product, and Company A delivers the product prior to the end of its current fiscal quarter. Company A's normal and customary business practice for this class of customer is to enter into a written sales agreement that requires the signatures of the authorized representatives of the Company and its customer to be binding. Company A prepares a written sales agreement, and its authorized representative signs the agreement before the end of the quarter. However, Customer B does not sign the agreement because Customer B is awaiting the requisite approval by its legal department. Customer B's purchasing department has orally agreed to the sale and stated that it is highly likely that the contract will be approved the first week of Company A's next fiscal quarter.

Analysis

Generally the staff believes that, in view of Company A's business practice of requiring a written sales agreement for this class of customer, persuasive evidence of an arrangement would require a final agreement that has been executed by the properly authorized personnel of the customer. In the staff's view, Customer Beta's execution of the sales agreement after the end of the quarter causes the transaction to be considered a transaction of the subsequent period. Further, if an arrangement is subject to subsequent approval (e.g., by the management committee or board of directors) or execution of another agreement, revenue recognition would be inappropriate until that subsequent approval or agreement is complete.

OPNET Technologies' revenue-recognition footnote is illustrative of how companies document and describe revenue arrangements.

OPNET Technologies, Inc. Form 10-K—March 31, 2012

Persuasive evidence of an arrangement exists

For license arrangements with end-users, it is the Company's customary practice to have a written software license agreement, which is signed by both the end user and the Company, and a purchase order or equivalent. A written contract can be executed based on the customer-specific format or on the standard "shrink wrap" software master license agreement. For those end users who have previously negotiated a software license agreement with the Company, the initial software license agreement is used as evidence of a written contract. Sales to distributors, resellers, and value-added resellers, which the Company collectively refers to as resellers, are evidenced by a master reseller agreement governing the relationship, which is signed by both the reseller and the Company, together with a purchase order on a transaction-by-transaction basis. To further evidence an arrangement, the Company's master reseller agreement requires that the reseller provide the Company copies of the end user's executed software master license agreements.

Delivery

The delivery criterion is met when the seller performs his or her obligations under the contract (explicit or implied). In determining revenue recognition, we need to make a distinction between delivery of products and delivery of services. Accountants generally use a separate model for products and services when recognizing revenue. For products, accountants generally use the Completed Performance model because value is delivered to the buyer when the products are delivered. (See Chapter 3: Product Revenue, which discusses this concept in detail.)

For services, the Proportional Performance model is generally used because the buyer is receiving value as each component of the service is being performed by the seller. For example, when a customer signs a contract to receive services from Verizon to utilize an iPhone for 24 months, we would record revenue as the services are delivered ratably over the 24 months in equal increments. (For additional guidance on accounting for service revenue transactions, see Chapter 4: Service Revenue.)

The following illustrates accounting guidance for complying with the delivery requirement for the recognition of revenue.

Fact Set

Company A receives purchase orders for products it manufactures. At the end of its fiscal quarters, customers may not yet be ready to take delivery of the products for various reasons. These reasons may include, but are not limited to, a lack of available space for inventory, having more than sufficient inventory in their distribution channels, or delays in customers' production schedules. The company clearly segregates the goods in its warehouse for future delivery for each customer order. Would the company be permitted to recognize revenue after the segregation of goods?

Analysis

Accounting guidance would normally conclude that delivery generally is not considered to have occurred unless the customer has taken title and assumed the risks and rewards of ownership of the products specified in the customer's purchase order or sales agreement. Typically this occurs when a product is delivered to the customer's delivery site (if the terms of the sale are "FOB destination") or when a product is shipped to the customer (if the terms are "FOB shipping point").

There are, however, circumstances if which these "bill and hold" revenue arrangements may result in companies being able to recognize revenue prior to shipment of goods to buyer. The following guidelines all must be met to qualify for revenue recognition.

1. The risks of ownership must have passed to the buyer.
2. The customer must have made a fixed commitment to purchase the goods, preferably in written documentation.
3. The buyer, not the seller, must request that the transaction be on a bill-and-hold basis. The buyer must have a substantial business purpose for ordering the goods on a bill-and-hold basis; such requests typically should be set forth in writing by the buyer.
4. There must be a fixed schedule for delivery of the goods. The date for delivery must be reasonable and must be consistent with the buyer's business purpose (e.g., storage periods are customary in the industry).
5. The seller must not have retained any specific performance obligations such that the earnings process is not complete.
6. The ordered goods must have been segregated from the seller's inventory and not be subject to being used to fill other orders.
7. The equipment [product] must be complete and ready for shipment.

Fixed or Determinable

Of the four cornerstones for revenue recognition, the fixed or determinable criterion is the most difficult to apply in determining the amount and timing of revenue to be recognized. Accounting guidance does not provide clear definitions for the fixed and determinable criterion. This places the company in the position of reasoning by analogy for each revenue transaction.[4] The difficulty in applying this principle of revenue recognition is in determining whether or not the revenue arrangement consideration could vary in the amount to be received by embedding contingent clauses in the sales contract.

Examples of contingent consideration to be received by the seller include: customer rights of return, volume discounts for additional

purchases, discounts on additional purchases, penalties for nonperform-
ance, bonus payments accruing to the seller for achieving performance
incentives.

In determining the variability of consideration to be received, there
have been numerous practice decisions made by the FASB and the SEC
that provide companies with accounting guidance. These decisions can
assist companies in meeting the fixed or determinable criteria for revenue
recognition. This accounting guidance is grouped into three four categories:

1. Customer Control
2. Seller's Control
3. Third-Party Control.

Customer Control

When determining the timing of the amount of revenue to be recognized
for actions that are within the control of the customer, the general rule
is to defer revenue until the customer exercises an action (option) that
determines for the company that the customer has taken control of the
product or service. For example:

Fact Set

Manufacturing Company sells customized equipment that is used to
produce machine parts. The company sells equipment to Precision
Company for a price of $500,000. The contract states that Precision[5]
Company has a right to return the equipment for a full refund if the
equipment does not meet its specifications. The contract also states
that this acceptance period ends after 60 days from date of delivery.

Analysis

In this case since the customer is in control of determining if
the equipment meets its specifications, the company would be
precluded from recognizing revenue until customer acceptance
has occurred or in 60 days after delivery provided the equipment
has not been returned.

There are, however, instances in which the seller can predict customer actions and has a reasonable basis in fact for doing so. The terminology used in accounting to describe those accounting estimates made by companies is called "breakage." In those circumstances, companies are allowed to predict actions that customers will or won't take and recognize revenue because the amount of revenue is considered determinable provided provisions are made that reduce revenue for the amount that is estimated to be not earned. This is a very powerful concept in revenue recognition. To repeat, provided companies have historical experience to make reliable estimates of actions their customers will or won't take, the company can recognize revenue on delivery or when the service is provided.

Learning Tree, Inc., revenue-recognition disclosure provides a very detailed evaluation of the concept of "breakage." The disclosure is also a very effective way to introduce revenue concepts that we will discuss in much greater detail in Chapter 3: Product Revenue and Chapter 4: Service Revenue.

Learning Tree 10-K for 2011

Revenue Recognition

We offer our customers a multiple-course sales discount referred to as a Learning Tree Training Passport. A Learning Tree Training Passport allows an individual Passport holder to attend up to a specified number of courses over a one- to two-year period for a fixed price. For a Training Passport, the amount of revenue recognized for each course attendance is based upon the selling price of the Training Passport, the list price of the course taken, the weighted average list price of all courses taken and the estimated average number of courses all Passport holders will actually attend. Upon expiration of each individual Training Passport, we record the difference, if any, between the revenues previously recognized and that specific Training Passport's total invoiced price. The estimated attendance rate is based upon the historical experience of the average number of course events that Training Passport holders have been attending. The actual Training Passport attendance rate is reviewed at least semiannually, and if the Training Passport attendance rates change, the revenue recognition rate for active Training Passports and for Training Passports sold thereafter is adjusted prospectively.

We believe it is appropriate to recognize revenues on this basis in order to most closely match revenue and related costs, as the substantial majority of our Passport holders do not attend the maximum number of course events permitted under their Training Passports. We believe that the use of recent historical data is reasonable and appropriate because of the relative stability of the average actual number of course events attended by Passport holders.

The average actual attendance rate for all expired Training Passports has closely approximated the estimated rate we utilize. Although we have seen no material changes in the historical rates as the number of course titles has changed, we monitor such potential effects. In general, determining the estimated average number of course events that will be attended by a Training Passport holder is based on historical trends that may not continue in the future. These estimates could differ in the near term from amounts used in arriving at the reported revenue. If the estimates are wrong, we would record the difference between the revenues previously recognized for that Training Passport and the Training Passport selling price upon expiration of that Training Passport. Thus, the timing of revenue recognition may be affected by an inaccurate estimation, but the inaccuracy would have no effect on the aggregate revenue recognized over the one- to two-year life of each Training Passport.

For newer Passport products for which historical utilization data is not available, we assume that the estimated average number of courses to be attended is equal to the number of courses available on the Passport. This assumed utilization rate may be revised in future periods after sufficient time has passed to amass historical trends.

Accounting guidance groups these breakage estimates when evaluating whether the revenue amount is fixed or determinable as return rights and rebate or coupon rights.

Specific Rights of Return

The accounting guidance for rights of return states that "revenue for products may be recognized on delivery as long as reliable estimates of returns can be made."[6] In order to arrive at a conclusion that the fixed and determinable criterion for revenue recognition is met for product returns; the company has to have sufficient historical evidence of homogeneous transactions for similar goods that have been sold to customers. If the company can produce a pattern of evidence of returns for products previously sold, the company would not be required to defer the revenue until the return period expires.

Coupons and Rebates

Manufacturing and retail companies in an effort to stimulate sales oftentimes offer coupons or rebates to customers. The general rule in revenue recognition is that embedding sales incentives in sales contracts is an indication that the revenue amount is not fixed or determinable. However, similar to accounting for rights of returns, if companies can reliably estimate the customer usage of coupons and rebates, then a company can record the revenue when the sale is made. The company also records an appropriate allowance for the rebate or coupon costs. For specific guidance for product and service companies, see Chapter 3: Product Revenue and Chapter 4: Service Revenue.

Abaxis, Inc., revenue recognition policy note from their 10-K for 2011 is illustrative of the types of revenue issues involved in accounting for rebates with customers.

The 10-K is a publicly held company's annual financial statement filing to the SEC.

Abaxis, Inc. 10-K for 2011

Distributor and Customer Rebates

We offer distributor pricing rebates and customer incentives, such as cash rebates, from time to time. The distributor pricing rebates are offered to distributors upon meeting the sales volume requirements during a qualifying period and are recorded as a reduction to gross revenues during a qualifying period. Cash rebates are offered to distributors or customers who purchase certain products or instruments during a promotional period and are recorded as a reduction to gross revenues.

The distributor pricing rebate program is offered to distributors in the North America veterinary market, upon meeting the sales volume requirements of veterinary products during the qualifying period. Factors used in the rebate calculations include the identification of products sold subject to a rebate during the qualifying period and which rebate percentage applies. Based on these factors and using historical trends, adjusted for current changes, we estimate the amount of the rebate that will be paid and record the liability as a reduction to gross revenues when we record the sale of the product. Settlement of the rebate accruals from the date of sale ranges from one to nine months after sale. Changes in the rebate accrual at each fiscal year end are based upon distributors meeting the purchase requirements during the quarter. Other rebate programs offered to distributors or customers vary from period to period in the medical and veterinary markets.

The following table summarizes the change in total accrued distributor and customer rebates (in thousands):

Year ended	Balance at beginning of year	Provisions	Payments	Balance at end of year
March 31, 2011	$48	$694	$331	$411
March 31, 2010	$96	$268	$316	$48
March 31, 2009	$140	$294	$338	$96

Sellers Control

In analyzing revenue transactions, in which the variable fees to be received are contingent of the seller's performance, it is generally "easier" for the seller to recognize revenue, than when predicting customer actions. This is because the company has more evidence of its own performance in delivering product and service deliverables to its customers.

For example, the seller agrees to refund a portion of the price paid by the buyer for a product if the seller's delivered cost price decreases. In this case, since the seller could estimate the price reduction, the seller would conclude that the price paid by the buyer is fixed or determinable.

Another example illustrates the condition when a firm has multiple products and services to be delivered. Mathews and Company sells precision tools to the independent construction contractors. A common revenue transaction is to deliver the product and provide training to customers on the use of the products. Since Mathews and Company has structured thousands of contracts similar to this, the company would conclude that it could deliver the training. The revenue is fixed and determinable.

Third-Party Actions

Actions taken by third parties that could result in the seller recording revenue are likely to be more difficult to predict than the actions that customers could take that would result in recording revenue for the seller. The general rule it that it is not appropriate to assume that third parties would take actions that would result in additional payments to the seller until they have occurred. For example, an operating lease may contain a contractual clause that would increase lease payments by the lessor (seller) if sales from use of the leased property exceed a contractual threshold. In this case, even if the historical sales numbers indicate a reasonable probability of the seller receiving the additional payments, revenue related to the additional payments would not be recognized until the specified sales level is achieved by sales to the third-party customers.

Actions taken by customers, companies, and third parties that would result in additional payments to the seller need to be analyzed when evaluating the fixed and determinable criteria for revenue recognition. Determinable revenue amounts that allow for revenue to be recorded involve the ability to predict actions that relate to variability of the revenue recorded. Accounting guidance makes it clear that if, and only if, the selling company has sufficient and reliable evidence of future actions of customers, companies, and third parties can the additional payments to be received be considered determinable for revenue-recognition purposes.

Collectability

The final criterion, when analyzing the earned and realizable concepts, is collectability. The application of this concept applies to companies that sell on credit and involves the likelihood of collection of the promised payment from the customer, which is usually called an account receivable. In revenue transactions, which lack a sufficiently high probability of collection (accounting guidance generally would say greater than or equal to 75%), revenue should be deferred until either the seller receives customer payments (cash accounting) or the probability of cash collection reaches the 75% threshold.

The revenue disclosure from Basset Furniture Industries is instructive as to the impact of collectability issues when recording and reporting revenue.

Bassett Furniture Industries, Inc. Form 10-K for **2010**

Staff Accounting Bulletin No. 104, *Revenue Recognition* ("SAB 104") outlines the four basic criteria for recognizing revenue as follows: (1) persuasive evidence of an arrangement exists, (2) delivery has occurred or services have been rendered, (3) the seller's price to the buyer is fixed or determinable, and (4) collectability is reasonably assured. SAB 104 further asserts that if collectability of all or a portion of the revenue is not reasonably assured, revenue recognition should be deferred until payment is received. During fiscal 2010, 2009 and 2008 there were seven, thirteen and five dealers, respectively, for which these criteria were not met and therefore revenue was being recognized on a cost recovery basis. As of November 27, 2010, November 28, 2009, and November 29, 2008 there were two, seven, and five dealers, respectively, that remained on the cost recovery basis. The following table details the total revenue and cost deferred:

	2010	2009	2008
Revenue deferred	$947	$7,149	$2,215
Cost deferred	$663	$5,004	$1,551

Excerpts from the revenue recognition footnotes of *IBM Corporation and Apple Corporation* for 2011 provide useful guidance on how those companies applied the four cornerstones of revenue recognition.

IBM Corporation 10K 2011

The company recognizes revenue when it is realized or realizable and earned. The company considers revenue realized or realizable and earned when it has persuasive evidence of an arrangement, delivery has occurred, the sales price is fixed or determinable and collectability is reasonably assured. Delivery does not occur until products have been shipped or services have been provided to the client, risk of loss has transferred to the client, and either client acceptance has been obtained, client acceptance provisions have lapsed, or the company has objective evidence that the criteria specified in the client acceptance provisions have been satisfied. The sales price is not considered to be fixed or determinable until all contingencies related to the sale have been resolved.

The company recognizes revenue on sales to solution providers, resellers and distributors (herein referred to as "resellers") when the reseller has economic substance apart from the company, credit risk, title and risk of loss to the inventory, the fee to the company is not contingent upon resale or payment by the end user, the company has no further obligations related to bringing about resale or delivery and all other revenue recognition criteria have been met.

Apple Corporation 10K for 2011

Net sales consist primarily of revenue from the sale of hardware, software, digital content and applications, peripherals, and service and support contracts. The Company recognizes revenue when persuasive evidence of an arrangement exists, delivery has occurred, the sales price is fixed or determinable, and collection is probable. Product is considered delivered to the customer once it has been shipped and title and risk of loss have been transferred. For most of the Company's product sales, these criteria are met at the time the product is shipped.

For online sales to individuals, for some sales to education customers in the United States, and for certain other sales, the Company defers revenue until the customer receives the product because the Company retains a portion of the risk of loss on these sales during transit.

The Company recognizes revenue from the sale of hardware products, software bundled with hardware that is essential to the functionality of the hardware, and third-party digital content sold on the iTunes Store in accordance with general revenue recognition accounting guidance. The Company recognizes revenue in accordance with industry specific software accounting guidance for the following types of sales transactions: (i) stand-alone sales of software products, (ii) sales of software upgrades and (iii) sales of software bundled with hardware not essential to the functionality of the hardware.

CHAPTER 2

Multiple-Element Arrangements

About This Chapter

Companies are increasingly offering bundled solutions in the form of products and services when selling to customers. These "bundled" solutions often involve multiple products or a combination of products and services. The packaging of multiple solutions to company's problems, which we will refer to as deliverables, results in two fundamental accounting issues in determining the amount of revenue to be recorded. Throughout the book, we will be referring to deliverables, elements, and obligations under multiple-element arrangements. These items are to be considered interchangeable.

1. Are the deliverables separate units of accounting for revenue-recognition purposes?
2. Since the sales contract will be negotiated as one price, how do we allocate a revenue amount to separate units of accounting?

This chapter presents a framework for analyzing revenue arrangements that involve multiple deliverables. The framework is comprised of the following components.

1. Identifying deliverables in an arrangement
2. Determining if the deliverables qualify as separate units of accounting
3. Determining the fixed or determinable transaction price
4. Allocating the fixed or determinable transaction price to the separate units of accounting to record revenue when that element is delivered

Identifying Deliverables

Accounting for revenue arrangements requires analysis on a transaction-by-transaction basis. This means that each arrangement that involves the company and the customer needs to be evaluated each time the company sells its products or services to each customer. Since companies tend to "bundle" multiple products/services when satisfying buyer demands, the crucial first step is to identify the item deliverables. The task is further complicated by the fact that accounting standard setters have not defined what constitutes a deliverable in accounting guidance, leaving it to companies to determine if their arrangement with customers contains multiple deliverables.

When performing your analysis of the number of deliverables, a useful methodology is to determine the number of obligations (promises) the seller has made to the buyer that is embodied in the sales contract. For example, Rodgers and Company promises to deliver products X, Y, and Z to the buyer as well as provide product support in marketing the products to customers. This arrangement has four deliverables (obligations). Deliver X, then Y, then Z, and product marketing support for each product delivered.

The aforementioned example also illustrates the difficulty in accounting properly for the delivered items in the arrangement. The delivery of products X, Y, and Z should pose no problems provided we can logically arrive at a price for each when sold separately or what we would charge customers if the products were sold separately. The difficulty comes into play when we evaluate the obligation to provide marketing support for the delivered products. Revenue recognition of product X may be deferred until we deliver the promised marketing support. The same would go for products X and Y. Another problem lies in determining the value of each of the four deliverables because the marketing support deliverable is connected to the three product deliverables.

The material in this chapter will equip you with the skill set to confidently analyze multiple-element arrangements as separate units of accounting to record the proper amount of revenue for each deliverable in compliance with the appropriate revenue-recognition guidance.

Determining Deliverables

In making the determination of the number of deliverables (obligations) in a revenue arrangement, we can use the following model:

- The obligation is explicitly referred to in the arrangement.
- Seller is required to perform a distinct action for the buyer.
- Seller's failure to perform an action would result in a contractual penalty for the seller.
- Inclusion or exclusion of an item in the arrangement would cause the transaction price to vary significantly (significantly implies that the total transaction price would vary by greater than or equal to 10%).

In addition to the company's offerings of products and services, revenue arrangements will frequently contain buyer options to purchase additional products or services. In analyzing deliverables as separate units of accounting, contractual terms indicating buyer rights to purchase additional products/services at below-market prices would generally indicate that those products/services are separate deliverables. In addition, the discount offered may be a separate deliverable that will affect the accounting for the other delivered products/services in the arrangement.

Accounting guidance provides criteria for determining when a discount on the purchase of future products represents a separate unit of accounting.[1]

More-than-insignificant discounts have all of the following characteristics:

1. Incremental to the range of discounts reflected in the pricing of the other elements of the arrangement.
2. Incremental to the range of discounts typically given in comparable transactions.
3. Significant if the discount or other concessions in an arrangement are more than insignificant; a presumption is created that an additional element or elements are being offered in the arrangement.

Judgment is required when assessing whether an incremental discount is significant.

To illustrate the accounting for discounts on additional purchases, consider the following.

Fact Set

A company sells products X and Y to customer for $200. X has a selling price of $120 and Y has an estimated selling price of $80. In addition, the company offers the customer a 50% discount on product Z, which has an estimated selling price of $170. The company normally offers a 25% discount on product Z to customers who purchase either X or Y.

Analysis

The price concession on product Z represents a 30% overall discount to the total consideration for the arrangement. Total consideration expected is $200 + $170 (0.5) = $285. The discount on Z is $170 (0.5) = $85. Overall discount is $285/$85 = 30%. The overall discount is significant for the arrangement. In addition, the discount is also incrementally significant compared to the discounts offered to other customers by 100%. (Calculations: discount of 25% (170) = and (85 − 42.5)/42.5 = 100%)

Companies, particularly in industries with fast-moving product changes, will often offer trade-in rights to its customers on future purchases of the next generation of the product. These options allow the customer, at some point in the future, to trade-in or return the purchased product with a corresponding percentage reduction of the original sales price on the new product purchased. Accounting guidance would treat the guarantee of the price reduction on the new product as a separate unit of accounting that would be recorded as a liability at the fair value of the guarantee. The following example illustrates the accounting guidance.

Fact Set

Electronics Company sells customer HD4 for $900. In the sales contract, the company will reduce the price of HD5 when purchased at 30% of the price paid for HD4 ($900 × 30% = $270).

Analysis

There are two deliverables and separate units of accounting in this arrangement: the product HD4 and the discount of $270 when the customer purchases HD5.

Note: the following format will be used throughout the book to indicate the accounting transaction impact on the financial statements.

Asset	= liabilities	+ shareholder's equity (SE) + Revenue – Expense

SE = increased by revenue and decreased by expenses and dividends paid

+ (plus) and the account title for an increase in the account balance

– (minus) and the account title for a decrease in the account

Record the sale of HD4

Asset	= liabilities	+ SE
Cash + 900	+ 270	+ 630 (revenue)

Guarantee liability would be recognized as revenue when the customer purchases HD5. The accounting would be:

	Guarantee liability: –270	+ 270 (revenue)

This would complete the accounting for the arrangement.

Note: Electronics Company, since the customer is not obligated to buy HD5, would likely convert a portion of the Guarantee Liability as revenue over a reasonable time period provided it has historical evidence that a percentage of customers do not avail themselves of the offer.

Separate Units of Accounting

The analysis after determining the number of deliverables continues with a determination of whether the deliverable qualifies as a separate unit of accounting. Accounting guidance has established two criteria for a delivered item to qualify as a separate unit of accounting in determining the amount of revenue to be recognized on delivery.[2]

1. The delivered item(s) has a stand-alone value to the customer.
2. If a general right of return exists, delivery or performance of the undelivered item(s) is substantially in the control of the vendor and is considered probable.

This analysis is the critical step in recognizing revenue for delivered items. Stand-alone value exists for a delivered item when:

1. Delivered item is sold separately
2. OR, the delivered item could be resold by the customer at a price that would substantially recover the original purchase price

Note: A substantial recovery would be at least 90% of the original purchase price.

Accounting guidance for the delivered item is sold separately extends to any company (competitors) that sells the item separately. In evaluating stand-alone value under option 2 above, the company would examine secondary markets (think Blue Book prices for equipment). When determining the stand-alone value by using a competitor's product or service offerings, companies will need to make adjustments in price if the competitor's offerings possess different product or service characteristics. The accounting guidance for using competitor pricing makes it clear that the products or services are interchangeable. (Caution: this can be a very difficult analysis since most companies differentiate their product and service offerings from competitors). In addition, companies would need to determine if the customer can use the deliverable for its intended purpose without receiving any additional deliverables from the company.

The revenue disclosure for Immunogen for the first quarter of 2011 is instructive of how a licensing company determines the stand-alone value for delivered items.

Immunogen, Inc., Form 10-Q for 2011

Exclusive licenses

The deliverables under an exclusive license agreement generally include the exclusive license to the Company's TAP technology, and may also include deliverables related to research activities to be performed on behalf of the collaborative partner and the manufacture of preclinical or clinical materials for the collaborative partner.

Generally, exclusive license agreements contain nonrefundable terms for payments and, depending on the terms of the agreement, provide that the Company will (i) at the collaborator's request, provide research services which are reimbursed at a contractually determined rate, (ii) at the collaborator's request, manufacture and provide to them preclinical and clinical materials which are reimbursed at the Company's cost, or, in some cases, cost plus a margin, (iii) earn payments upon the achievement of certain milestones and (iv) earn royalty payments, generally until the later of the last applicable patent expiration or 10 to 12 years after product launch. Royalty rates may vary over the royalty term depending on the Company's intellectual property rights. The Company may provide technical assistance and share any technology improvements with its collaborators during the term of the collaboration agreements. The Company does not directly control when any collaborator will request research or manufacturing services, achieve milestones or become liable for royalty payments. As a result, the Company cannot predict when it will recognize revenues in connection with any of the foregoing. In determining the units of accounting, management evaluates whether the exclusive license has standalone value to the collaborative partner based on the consideration of the relevant facts and circumstances for each arrangement. Factors considered in this determination include the research capabilities of the partner and the availability of TAP technology research expertise in the general marketplace.

Novartis

In October 2010, the Company entered into an agreement with Novartis Institutes for BioMedical Research, Inc. (Novartis). The agreement initially provides Novartis with a research license to test the Company's TAP technology with Novartis' own antibodies and an option to take exclusive development and commercialization licenses to use ImmunoGen's TAP technology to develop therapeutic products for a specified number of individual antigen targets. The initial term of the research license is for three years and it may be extended by Novartis for up to two one-year periods by the payment of additional consideration. The terms of the agreement also require Novartis to exercise its option for the development and commercialization licenses by the end of the research term. The Company received a $45 million up-front payment in connection with the execution of the agreement, and for each development and commercialization license for an antigen target, the Company is entitled to receive milestone payments potentially totaling $200.5 million plus royalties on product sales, if any. The Company also is entitled to receive payments for manufacturing preclinical and clinical materials at the request of Novartis as well as for research and development activities performed on behalf of Novartis. Novartis is responsible for the development, manufacturing, and marketing of any products resulting from this agreement.

In accordance with Accounting Standards Update ASU No. 2009–13, the Company identified all of the deliverables at the inception of the agreement. The significant deliverables were determined to be the research license, the exclusive development and commercialization licenses and the research services. The Company has determined that the research license together with the development and commercialization licenses represent one unit of accounting as the research license does not have stand-alone value from the development and commercialization licenses. The Company has also determined that this unit of accounting does have standalone value from the research services. As a result, the research services are considered a separate unit of accounting. The estimated selling prices for these units of accounting was determined based on market conditions and entity-specific factors such as the terms of the Company's previous collaborative agreements, recent preclinical and clinical testing results of therapeutic products that use the Company's TAP technology, the Company's pricing practices and pricing objectives, and the nature of the research services to be performed for Novartis and market rates for similar services. The arrangement consideration was allocated to the deliverables based on the relative selling price method. The Company will recognize license revenue as each exclusive development and commercialization license is delivered pursuant to the terms of the agreement. The Company does not control when Novartis will exercise its options for development and commercialization licenses. As a result, the Company cannot predict when it will recognize the related license revenue except that it will be within the term of the research license. The Company will recognize research services revenue as the related services are delivered.

Application of the second criterion to qualify as a separate unit of accounting (seller is substantially in control of delivery or performance for the undelivered items) is necessary to ensure that the arrangement consideration is fixed or determinable. In making an assessment of "substantially in control," accounting guidance indicates that the threshold for arriving at this conclusion for undelivered items is "more likely than not" (i.e., greater than a 50% probability of occurring). Companies that routinely deliver goods and services without difficulty will have sufficient evidence to meet the substantially in control requirement.

Accounting guidance offers the following factors to assist companies in determining whether delivery is probable and substantially in control of the seller.[3]

- The amount of time to complete the arrangement
- The degree of customization of the product or service
- The reliance the company places on subcontractors

- The availability of components
- The vendor's history of performance and financial condition must also be considered in the assessment.

When companies regularly sell extended maintenance contracts, in addition to the standard warranty, which are separately priced, we would treat them as a separate unit of accounting[4] and not as a deliverable in an arrangement that would require allocation of the consideration received to the other deliverables in the arrangement. An extended warranty or maintenance contract is an agreement to provide warranty protection in addition to the scope of coverage of the manufacturer's original warranty, if any, or to extend the period of coverage provided by the manufacturer's original warranty. For example, Company sells equipment and provides installation services and offers an extended 5-year maintenance contract that is separately priced. In this case, we would treat the equipment and installation as two deliverables in an arrangement. We would treat the extended maintenance contract as a separate deliverable and not part of the arrangement.

It is, however, important to note that failure to qualify under the stand-alone value criteria or the substantially in control of the seller criteria means that the company has one unit of accounting for its deliverables in the arrangement. In that case, the last delivered item will determine the appropriate revenue-recognition guidance to use. (See Chapter 3—Product Revenue and Chapter 4—Service Revenue)

Inconsequential or Perfunctory Deliverables

When performing an analysis of the number of deliverables contained in the revenue arrangement in order to determine which deliverables will be separate units of accounting, the guidance refers to "substantially complete or fulfill the terms specified in the arrangement."[5] The practical interpretation of this is that not all deliverables will be accounted for as separate units of accounting and revenue recognition may not be delayed even if other deliverables have not been delivered to the buyer.

Accounting guidance for applying the substantially complete concept is that those deliverables in the revenue arrangement that are inconsequential or perfunctory to value passing to the buyer should not impede the recognition of revenue. However, if failure to complete a deliverable, even if inconsequential or perfunctory, would result in a refund or cancellation of the revenue transactions, then those deliverables cannot be considered inconsequential or perfunctory. The reasoning is that in the case of a refund, the earnings process would not be complete until the delivery is performed or in the case where cancellation value has not passed to the buyer and the seller has continuing involvement in the revenue arrangement.

Accounting guidance[6] lists factors that any remaining performance obligation (deliverable) is substantive and not inconsequential or perfunctory. These factors are:

The seller does not have a demonstrated history of completing the remaining tasks in a timely manner and reliably estimating their costs.

The cost or time to perform the remaining obligations for similar contracts historically has varied significantly from one instance to another.

The skills or equipment required to complete the remaining activity are specialized or are not readily available in the marketplace.

The cost of completing the obligation, or the fair value of that obligation, is more than insignificant in relation to such items as the contract fee, gross profit, and operating income allocable to the unit of accounting.

The period before the remaining obligation will be extinguished is lengthy. Registrants should consider whether reasonably possible variations in the period to complete performance affect the certainty that the remaining obligations will be completed successfully and on budget.

The timing of payment of a portion of the sales price is coincident with completing performance of the remaining activity.

Registrants' determinations of whether remaining obligations are inconsequential or perfunctory should be consistently applied.

Accounting guidance for revenue arrangements in which the deliverable would be considered inconsequential or perfunctory would include:
the equipment is a standard product;

Installation does not significantly alter the equipment's usefulness to the buyer;

Other companies could perform the installation.

Measurement and Allocation Guidance

Our measurement challenge for the consideration received is complicated by two factors.

1. accounting for contingent (variable) fees in an arrangement;
2. allocating discounts to the deliverables in the arrangement.

The process of allocating contingent fees for a revenue arrangement involves arriving at a conclusion as to whether or not the consideration to be received is fixed or determinable. When performing this analysis, companies are guided by three "rules" as established by accounting standard setters.

1. Customers will only purchase the contractual minimum amount of products and services in the arrangement.
2. Performance bonuses should not be included in allocable consideration to be received until those payments have been earned.
3. Amounts received by the seller if the customer terminates the arrangement (cancellation penalty) shall not be included in allocable consideration.

To illustrate these concepts assume the following.

Fact Set

A seller enters into an arrangement with a buyer to provide equipment and a service contract on maintaining the equipment for a 5-year period after delivery of the equipment. The buyer agrees to pay $4,000,000 for the two deliverables, which are considered separate units of accounting. In addition, the contractual terms state the following:

- The buyer agrees to pay the seller a 3% bonus for products manufactured and sold with the purchased equipment that exceed sales of $30,000,000 per year (12 calendar months). The seller has no relevant experience of this particular option with other customers.
- If the buyer achieves a 98% defect-free rate of products manufactured with the equipment, the seller will receive a bonus of $50,000 per year (12 months).
- If the buyer cancels the service contract at any time, the seller receives a $250,000 payment from the buyer.

Analysis

Arrangement consideration is $4,000,000 for the two deliverables. The additional income, bonus payments, and cancellation penalty will be accounted for as separate units of accounting when they occur.

Allocation Guidance

Arrangement consideration to be received from the buyer shall be allocated to separate deliverables (separate units of accounting) based on the relative-sales-price-method. Accounting guidance for allocating arrangement consideration mandates the use of a three-tiered model.[7]

1. Vendor-specific objective evidence (VSOE)—the price at which the company regularly sells the item on a stand-alone basis (price sold separately)
2. Third-party evidence (TPE)—When VSOE does not exist, then companies can use competitor pricing of similar products/services with price adjustments for the particular value attributes of the product/service deliverables as compared to those of the competitors.
3. Best estimate of selling price (BESP)—When neither VSOE nor TPE is available, sellers can determine their own BESP based on available market evidence of what products/services would sell for in orderly markets. The BESP is a proxy for the stand-alone value of the deliverable; that is, what is the price if the separate unit of accounting would be sold separately.

VSOE

When establishing VSOE, the vendor (seller) needs to perform a VSOE analysis. The purpose of the analysis is to provide evidence that a substantial majority of the recent stand-alone sales of a product or service is within a relatively narrow range. For example, recent stand-alone sales of a product are within a range of 15% of the midpoint. An item priced at $1,000 has sold between $850 and $1,150 for 85% of the most recent transactions. Accounting guidance indicates that the low point of the range should be VSOE, although the midpoint can be used if more representative of the actual price paid by customers. The analysis relative dispersion of sales prices around the mean (average) will indicate to the company the appropriate VSOE to use in multiple-element arrangements.

TPE

If the seller cannot establish VSOE of the selling price, then the company needs to analyze whether there is TPE by the company's competitor's offerings that would establish a selling price's stand-alone value. This particular analysis is more qualitative than determining VSOE with the following factors guiding your decision making.

- Comparisons with similar or identical items for similar customers.
- Items sold by third parties are largely interchangeable and can be used in similar situations by similar customers.
- The degree of customization needs to be considered by the seller.
- When the item is a service, then factors include length of time to complete the service and the level and skill necessary to perform the service.

The use of TPE to arrive at the stand-alone value for the seller is a matter of professional judgment given the facts and circumstances that exist at the time.

BESP

When the seller can neither determine VSOE or TPE, the company may determine its own BSEP. The objective remains the same: at what price would the seller sell the item to a customer if the product/service were sold separately. When making this determination, companies would consider both market-pricing information and its own assumptions about pricing. Market data about pricing would include:

- What is competitor pricing for a similar product?
- What are the company's market share and position (ability to dictate pricing)?
- How does customization affect pricing?
- What are the current market trends for pricing of similar products?

Entity-specific factors would include:

- profit objectives for the good or service and cost structure to produce a product or service;
- pricing objectives for selling bundled products/services;
- whether size of customer or size of the deal affects pricing objectives.

Companies using the BESP to get the stand-alone value would be wise to gather as much pertinent evidence as is practicable and have established routines for determining the "proxy" price of an item if sold separately. There are two exceptions to the relative-sales-price-method that will apportion the discount proportionately to the deliverables under the law of one price. These are: first, when a separate unit of accounting in an arrangement is to be accounted for at the fair value under other accounting guidance, then that deliverable is not allocated any discount and is instead recorded at the fair value. For example, the presence of a guarantee by a third party that the seller's products will meet customer specifications for performance would be a separate unit of accounting and recorded at fair value in the arrangement.

Second, arrangement consideration that is otherwise allocable to a separate unit of accounting is limited to the lesser of the amount that is not contingent on the seller's delivery of other items or if meeting a specified performance obligation.

Fact Set

A seller agrees to deliver products X, Y, and Z to a buyer. The following table contains the required information.

Product	$ Price (cash received)	$ BESP
X	150	180
Y	275	260
Z	180	185
Total	605	625

Analysis

The allocation of revenue using the relative-sales-price-method would be as follows for separate unit of accounting X.

$$\$605/\$625 \times \$180 = \$174.24$$

However, the amount of revenue to be recorded after delivery of X is limited to the lesser of the amount that is not contingent on the seller's delivery of Y and Z. In this case, revenue for X would be limited to $150, which is derived from the total consideration to be received of $605 minus the consideration to be received for delivery of Y (275) plus Z ($180) which would equal $455. The cash to be received for delivery of Y and Z.

The recording of the aforementioned transaction in the financial statements would be

Asset	= liabilities	+ SE
cash + 150 + receivable + 24.24	24.24 (deferred revenue)	+ 150 (revenue)

The deferred revenue would become earned revenue when we deliver Y and Z.

BESP for Discounts

The right to a discount on future purchases of goods and services by the customer, if incremental to other discounts offered to regular customers or significant in relation to the overall consideration transferred, qualifies as a separate unit of accounting. Accounting guidance indicates that the preferred methodology when allocating consideration to the separate units of accounting in a multiple-element arrangement would be the BESP. The following example illustrates the accounting for such an arrangement.

Fact Set

A seller enters into an arrangement with a buyer to sell Product X and Service Y for a consideration of $150,000. In addition, the seller offers the buyer a $25,000 discount on product Z with the offer good for 1 year from delivery of product X. The buyer concludes that the discount is incremental to other buyers of their products and services and is significant in relation to the overall arrangement and, therefore, qualifies as a separate unit of accounting.

Analysis

Seller would allocate consideration to product X and Service Y and the discount on Z. (*Note*: the amount allocated to the discount deliverable would be deferred until the customer orders product Z). Assume that we assign BESP for product X of $110,000, service Y of $70,000, and the discount at $20,000. The allocation of the $150,000 consideration received would be

Item	BESP ($)	Allocation (%)	Price ($)	Amount ($)
Product X	110,000	55	150,000	82,500
Service Y	70,000	35	150,000	52,500
Discount on Z	20,000	10	150,000	15,000
Total	200,000	100		150,000

Asset	= liabilities	+ SE

Accounting for the delivery of product X and service Y:

+Cash + 150,000	+ deferred revenue + 15,000	+ revenue + 135,000

Buyer exercises option to purchase product Z:

	−deferred revenue $15,000	+ revenue + 15,000

The following two examples of revenue-recognition disclosures for multiple-deliverable arrangements illustrate most of the concepts we have discussed in this chapter.

IBM 10-K for 2011

The company enters into revenue arrangements that may consist of multiple deliverables of its products and services based on the needs of its clients. These arrangements may include any combination of services, software, hardware and/or financing. For example, a client may purchase a server that includes operating system software. In addition, the arrangement may include postcontract support for the software and a contract for postwarranty maintenance service for the hardware. These types of arrangements can also include financing provided by the company. These arrangements consist of multiple deliverables, with the hardware and software delivered in one reporting period and the software support and hardware maintenance services delivered across multiple reporting periods. In another example, a client may outsource the running of its data-center operations to the company on a long-term, multiple-year basis and periodically purchase servers and/or software products from the company to upgrade or expand its facility. The outsourcing services are provided on a continuous basis across multiple reporting periods and the hardware and software products are delivered in one reporting period. To the extent that a deliverable in a multiple-deliverable arrangement is subject to specific guidance that deliverable is accounted for in accordance with such specific guidance. Examples of such arrangements may include leased hardware which is subject to specific leasing guidance or software which is subject to specific software revenue

recognition guidance (see "VSOE" on page 32) on whether and/
or how to separate multiple-deliverable arrangements into separate units of accounting (separability) and how to allocate the
arrangement consideration among those separate units of accounting (allocation). For all other deliverables in multiple-deliverable
arrangements, the guidance below is applied for separability and
allocation. A multiple-deliverable arrangement is separated into
more than one unit of accounting if the following criteria are met:

1. The delivered item(s) has value to the client on a stand-alone
   basis; and
2. If the arrangement includes a general right of return relative to
   the delivered item(s), delivery or performance of the undelivered
   item(s) is considered probable and substantially in the control of
   the company.

   If these criteria are not met, the arrangement is accounted for
as one unit of accounting which would result in revenue being
recognized ratably over the contract term or being deferred until
(1) the earlier of when the two criterion above are met or (2) when
the last undelivered element is delivered. If these criteria are met
for each element and there is a relative selling price for all units
of accounting in an arrangement, the arrangement consideration
is allocated to the separate units of accounting based on each
unit's relative selling price. The following revenue policies are then
applied to each unit of accounting, as applicable.
   Revenue from the company's business analytics, smarter
planet and cloud offerings follow the specific revenue recognition
policies for multiple deliverable arrangements and for each major
category of revenue depending on the type of offering which can
be comprised of services, hardware and/or software.

Apple 10K for 2011

For multielement arrangements that include hardware products
containing software essential to the hardware product's functionality, undelivered software elements that relate to the hardware product's essential software, and undelivered non-software

services, the Company allocates revenue to all deliverables based on their relative selling prices. In such circumstances, the Company uses a hierarchy to determine the selling price to be used for allocating revenue to deliverables: (i) vendor-specific objective evidence of fair value ("VSOE"), (ii) third-party evidence of selling price ("TPE"), and (iii) best estimate of selling price ("ESP"). VSOE generally exists only when the Company sells the deliverable separately and is the price actually charged by the Company for that deliverable. ESPs reflect the Company's best estimates of what the selling prices of elements would be if they were sold regularly on a stand-alone basis. For multielement arrangements accounted for in accordance with industry specific software accounting guidance, the Company allocates revenue to all deliverables based on the VSOE of each element, and if VSOE does not exist revenue is recognized when elements lacking VSOE are delivered.

For sales of qualifying versions of iPhone, iPad, and iPod touch ("iOS devices"), Mac and Apple TV, the Company has indicated it may from time to time provide future unspecified software upgrades and features to the essential software bundled with each of these hardware products free of charge to customers. Essential software for iOS devices includes iOS and related applications and for Mac includes OS X, related applications and iLife. The Company also provides various nonsoftware services to owners of qualifying versions of iOS devices and Mac. The Company has identified up to three deliverables regularly included in arrangements involving the sale of these devices. The first deliverable is the hardware and software essential to the functionality of the hardware device delivered at the time of sale. The second deliverable is the embedded right included with the purchase of iOS devices, Mac, and Apple TV to receive on a when-and-if-available basis, future unspecified software upgrades and features relating to the product's essential software. The third deliverable is the nonsoftware services to be provided to qualifying versions of iOS devices and Mac. The Company allocates revenue between these deliverables using the relative selling price method. Because the Company has neither VSOE nor TPE for these deliverables, the allocation of revenue is based on the Company's ESPs. Revenue allocated to the delivered hardware and the related essential software is recognized at the time of sale provided the other conditions for revenue recognition have been met. Revenue allocated to the embedded unspecified software upgrade rights and the nonsoftware services is deferred and recognized on a straight-line basis over the estimated period the software upgrades and non-software services are expected to be provided for each of these devices, which ranges from two to four years. Cost of sales related to delivered hardware and related essential software, including estimated warranty costs, are recognized at the time of sale. Costs incurred to provide nonsoftware services are recognized as cost of sales as incurred, and engineering and sales and marketing costs are recognized as operating expenses as incurred.

The Company's process for determining its ESP for deliverables without VSOE or TPE considers multiple factors that may vary depending upon the unique facts and circumstances related to each deliverable. The Company believes its customers would be reluctant to buy unspecified software upgrade rights for the essential software included with its qualifying hardware products. This view is primarily based on the fact that unspecified software upgrade rights do not obligate the Company to provide upgrades at a particular time or at all, and do not specify to customers which upgrades or features will be delivered. The Company also believes its customers would be unwilling to pay a significant amount for access to the nonsoftware services because other companies offer similar services at little or no cost to users. Therefore, the Company has concluded that if it were to sell upgrade rights or access to the nonsoftware services on a stand-alone basis, including those rights and services attached to iOS devices, Mac, and Apple TV, the selling prices would be relatively low. Key factors considered by the Company in developing the ESPs for software upgrade rights include prices charged by the Company for similar offerings, market trends in the pricing of Apple-branded and third-party

Mac and iOS compatible software, the nature of the upgrade rights (e.g., unspecified versus specified), and the relative ESP of the upgrade rights as compared to the total selling price of the product.

The Company may also consider additional factors as appropriate, including the impact of other products and services provided to customers, the pricing of competitive alternatives if they exist, product-specific business objectives, and the length of time a particular version of a device has been available. When relevant, the same factors are considered by the Company in developing ESPs for offerings such as the nonsoftware services; however, the primary consideration in developing ESPs for the nonsoftware services is the estimated cost to provide such services, including consideration for a reasonable profit margin.

For the three years ended September 29, 2012, the Company's combined ESPs for the unspecified software upgrade rights and the rights to receive the nonsoftware services included with its qualifying hardware devices have ranged from $5 to $25. Revenue allocated to such rights included with iOS devices and Apple TV is recognized on a straight-line basis over two years, and revenue allocated to such rights included with Mac is recognized on a straight-line basis over four years.

Comprehensive Examples from the Accounting Standards Codification (ASC) Adapted for Our Purposes[8]

Sale of Home Appliances with Installation and Maintenance Services—Presence of VSOE and TPE

Fact Set

A company is an experienced home appliance dealer and retailer. The company regularly sells its appliances on a stand-alone basis. The company also sells installation and maintenance services for its appliances. However, the company does not sell installation and maintenance services on appliances sold by competitors.

Assume that the company's pricing menu for appliance X is as follows:

- Appliance X only: $800
- Appliance X with installation services: $850
- Appliance X with maintenance services: $975
- Appliance X with maintenance and installation services: $1,000

The pricing structure is $50 for installation, which approximates the market price charged by competitors for this product. The installation service is separately priced in the arrangement at $175.

The appliance is sold with a general right of return. If the company does not satisfactorily complete installation and maintenance, the customer is entitled to a refund of the price paid that exceeds $800.

The customer purchases the appliance with the two service contracts for $1,000. The company concludes that since the maintenance services are priced separately, they qualify as a separate unit of accounting. The company also has a history of successful installations. The company is trying to determine if the appliance and installation services are separate units of accounting.

Analysis

The first condition for separation (stand-alone value) is met because the company regularly sells the appliance separately without including the service components. The second criterion (substantially in control of the other deliverables in the arrangement) is also met because even though a general right of return exists, the company has evidence that it can successfully perform installation. The appliance and the installation are separate units of accounting.

The company would allocate $175 of the arrangement consideration to the maintenance contract, leaving $825 to be allocated to the other deliverables.

Note: the company does not consider the contingency of not satisfactorily performing the installation services when allocating consideration received to the remaining separate units of accounting.

The following table illustrates the allocation.

Items	Selling price ($)	Consideration ($) for the arrangement	Consideration % for the arrangement	Revenue amount ($)
Appliance	800	825	94	776
Installation	50	825	6	49
Total	850	$	100	825

In this case, we have Vendor Specific Objective Evidence (VSOE) for the appliance since it is sold separately and TPE for the installation since others offer the service at that price.

Note: since the refund relates only to the installation, it is not germane to the recording of revenue of the appliance.

Revenue recognition for the appliance would occur when the product is delivered. As for the installation, revenue of $49 would be recognized when it is completed and the customer is satisfied as to installation.

Sale of Human Resources (HR) Services—Applying the BESP

Fact Set

A company provides its customers with a suite of HR solutions including employee relations, payroll and tax services, benefit consulting, and administration. Customers can do one of the following:

- choose a prepackaged bundle of services;
- customize and existing bundle of services;
- select the individual services they need.

Because customers need different HR services, no two arrangements are exactly the same. The company prices its services on the unique bundle of services provided to customers. Because of the customization of the services, the company does not have VSOE for any particular bundle of products and the company is unable to gather sufficient information from competitors to determine TPE.

On January 2, X1, the company enters into an arrangement with customers to provide HR solution services under a 3-year contract. Services to be provided include:

- Payroll processing
- Three periodic training events to be provided annually
- Executive compensation assessment to be completed by June 30, X1
- Employee Handbook to be completed by June 30, X2.

Total compensation under the arrangement is $1,275,000. Payments by customer consist of: $375,000 up-front and monthly payments of $25,000.

An evaluation by the company determines that they have four separate units of accounting:

- Payroll processing
- Periodic training
- Employee handbook development
- Executive compensation assessment.

The company determines that the four deliverables have a stand-alone value, but they have neither VSOE nor TPE for any of the deliverables; so the company will employ BESP for allocating consideration to the separate units of accounting.

In making the determination of the stand-alone value of the separate units of accounting, the company will follow its pricing practice of applying a gross profit margin percentage to the costs of providing each deliverable. The pricing of bundled services has been developed over time on the basis of available market demand and data for the services. The company has developed the following gross margin percentages of its deliverables:

- A 26% profit margin on its payroll-processing services
- A 15% gross margin on its employee handbook development service and its executive compensation service
- A 22% gross margin on its training services before considering any discount on the total arrangement.

Analysis

Using company-specific estimates of the costs for each service delivered and its relevant gross margin percentages, the company estimated the stand-alone selling price for its deliverables as follows.

Determining the best estimate of selling price (BESP)	$ BESP
Costs to be incurred for payroll-processing for 3 years	976,250
1. Payroll gross profit margin of 26%	Divided by 0.74
Estimated selling price for payroll processing	1,319,257
Estimated costs for the executive compensation assessment	45,223
2. Executive compensation gross margin of 15%	Divided by 0.85
Estimated selling price of executive compensation assessment	53,204
Estimated costs for the employee handbook	56,113
3. Employee handbook gross margin of 15%	Divided by 0.85
Estimated selling price of employee handbook	66,015
Estimated costs for the 3 training events	40,708
4. Training event gross margin of 22%	Divided by 0.78
Estimated selling price of 3 training events	52,187
Total estimated selling prices of the deliverables	1,490,663

The next step is to allocate the separate units of accounting based on the total consideration to be received of $1,275,000.

Deliverable/ element	Calculation to arrive at amount recorded	$ Amount recorded
Payroll processing	(1,275,000) (1,319,257/1,490,663)	$1,128,392
Executive compensation	(1,275,000) (53,024/1,490,663)	$45,507
Employee handbook	(1,275,000) (66,015/1,490,663)	$56,464
Training events	(1,275,000) (52,187/1,460,663)	$44,367
Total consideration		$1,275,000

Revenue recognition for the payroll processing would be recognized ratably over the 36 months of the contract. The executive compensation and the employee handbook deliverables would generally be recognized when they are delivered. The training deliverable would be recognized ratably when they are delivered. It is worth noting that the $375,000 up-front payment would be deferred over the life of the contract and released to revenue when the separate units of accounting are performed for the customer.

Asset	= liabilities	+ SE + Revenue – Expenses

Record cash payment received to start the arrangement

+ Cash +375,000	+ deferred revenue + 375,000	

To record cash payments received per contractual term. This entry will be made another 35 times, resulting in a deferred revenue of $900,000. This amount when added to the up-front payments will equal $1,275,000.

+ Cash + 25,000	+ deferred revenue + 25,000	

To record 1 month's revenue for payroll processing. This entry will be made 35 more times to arrive at the total revenue for payroll of $1,128,392.

	– deferred revenue – 31,344	+ revenue + 31,344

To record revenue for the executive compensation assessment when it is delivered on June 30, X1

	– deferred revenue + 45,507	+ revenue + 45,507

To record revenue for the employee handbook when it is delivered on June 30, X2

	– deferred revenue + 56,464	+ revenue + 56,464

To record revenue after completing the first training event. This entry will be recorded two more times resulting in a total of $44,637

	– deferred revenue + 14,879	+ revenue + 14,879

CHAPTER 3

Product Revenue

About This Chapter

Product revenue is earned when the risk and rewards of ownership substantially transfer from the seller to the buyer. This transfer is usually accompanied by the transfer of legal title to the products; so from an accounting and legal perspective, the revenue has been earned on delivery. Companies would use the Completed Performance model for revenue recognition, provided the seller has no continuing involvement with the product. There are, however, issues of continuing involvement, such as rights of return, product warranties, customer acceptance provisions, which can make the accounting more complex.

As discussed in Chapter 1, the four principles of revenue recognition are:

1. Persuasive evidence of an arrangement exists.
2. Delivery or performance has occurred.
3. The arrangement consideration is fixed or determinable.
4. Collectability is reasonably assured.

This chapter will build on the principles of revenue recognition while allowing us a deeper dive into rights of return, product warranties, and other issues regarding product revenue.

Risks and Rewards of Ownership

Risks of ownership refer to all of the downside risks that buyers incur from purchasing a product. These risks would include loss of market value, inventory obsolescence, theft, physical damage, and excess inventory. Rewards from ownership are the right to increase in market value, the right to use the product or to restrict its use, and the right to grant security interests in the property.

The risks and rewards of ownership generally transfer to the buyer at delivery. In addition, the seller would generally transfer title to the buyer when the products are delivered. The party that has the property "title" is assumed to control the product use and be subject to gain or loss from the use of that product. However, there are contractual arrangements in which the transfer of title to the customer does not transfer the risks and rewards of ownership. For example, a manufacturer sells to a retailer 1,000 units of product X. The manufacturer also grants the buyer a right to return any unsold goods for a 90-day period after delivery. The presence of the return rights may indicate that the seller's continuing involvement in the transaction prevents revenue recognition until there has been "sell through" to third parties. This would be the case even if title was transferred on delivery of the product.

Another complication in the timing of revenue recognition occurs when the seller uses a third party to transport goods. The question is the same: When does the buyer assume substantially the risks and rewards of ownership? Accounting guidance in this area is called Free-on-Board (FOB). FOB Shipping Point means the transportation cost is paid by the buyer, and therefore, revenue recognition occurs when products are loaded on board the transport vehicle, because the buyer has risk of loss in transit. (Note that this is the case even if the company has its own fleet of vehicles.) FOB Destination indicates that the risk of loss remains with the seller until the goods are delivered to the buyer's location. Shipping terms would normally be specified contractually.

As a practical matter, most companies record revenue when the goods leave the seller's premises, regardless of contractual shipping terms. This is done because it is easier for companies to determine when goods leave their locations, than it is to determine when delivery occurs to the buyer. If companies do not have risk of loss in transit they would be required to reverse any revenue recorded that has not yet arrived at the buyer's location.

Another issue occurs when the seller delivers the product to a third party prior to its delivery to the final customer. If the seller retains continuing involvement, such as assuring that payment will be refunded if not delivered in 3 days, then the revenue for that transaction is delayed until delivery to the final customer has occurred.

Continuing Involvement After Delivery

Consignment sales are not sales at all, because the risk of loss continues to be absorbed by the seller, until the "buyer" sells through to the final customer. Therefore, a shipment of goods on consignment does not meet the delivery requirement under the earned criteria for revenue recognition.[1] When a contractual agreement between buyer and seller transfers product title, but grants the buyer an unlimited right of return and payment is not due until the products are sold through to the final customer, we have what is called "in-substance" consignment. Accounting guidance lists the following as qualitative guidance in determining if a revenue arrangement is an "in-substance" consignment.[2]

- Payment is not due to the "seller" until the products have been sold to a third party.
- The buyer uses financing or guarantees from the seller to purchase the products (product financing arrangement).
- The buyer possesses an unlimited right of return (buyer has no risk of loss).
- Seller imposes business constraints on the buyer regarding pricing, credit policies, and the like (indicates that rewards of ownership have not transferred).
- Seller assumes the credit risk for sales to the final customer (buyer is an agent for the seller).

The aforementioned list is not meant to be all inclusive. The analysis for recording revenue on delivery remains the same. If the seller has continuing involvement with the buyer and the eventual final customer, revenue recognition may be delayed until the continuing involvement is extinguished.

The following revenue disclosure for Advanced Micro Devices Corporation for 2011 is instructive in accounting for "in-substance" consignments.

Advanced Micro Devices, Inc., 10-K for 2011

Revenue recognition. The Company recognizes revenue from products sold directly to customers, including original equipment

manufacturers (OEMs), when persuasive evidence of an arrangement exists, the price is fixed or determinable, delivery has
occurred and collectability is reasonably assured. Estimates of
product returns, allowances, and future price reductions, based on
actual historical experience and other known or anticipated trends
and factors, are recorded at the time revenue is recognized. The
Company sells to distributors under terms allowing the majority
of distributors certain rights of return and price protection on
unsold merchandise held by them. The distributor agreements,
which may be cancelled by either party upon specified notice, generally contain a provision for the return of those of the Company's
products that the Company has removed from its price book or
that are not more than twelve months older than the manufacturing code date. In addition, some agreements with distributors
may contain standard stock rotation provisions permitting limited
levels of product returns. Therefore the Company is unable to estimate the product returns and pricing when the product is sold to
the distributors. Accordingly, the Company defers the gross margin resulting from the deferral of both revenue and related product costs from sales to distributors with agreements that have the
aforementioned terms until the merchandise is resold by the distributors and reports such deferred amounts as "Deferred income
on shipments to distributors" on its consolidated balance sheet.
Products are sold to distributors at standard published prices that
are contained in price books that are broadly provided to the
Company's various distributors. Distributors are then required to
pay for these products within the Company's standard commercial terms, which are typically net 30 days. The Company records
allowances for price protection given to distributors and customer
rebates in the period of distributor re-sale. The Company determines these allowances based on specific contractual terms with
its distributors. Price reductions generally do not result in sales
prices that are less than the Company's product cost. Deferred
income on shipments to distributors is revalued at the end of each
period based on the change in inventory units at distributors, latest published prices, and latest product costs.

The Company also sells its products to distributors under sales arrangements whose terms do not allow for rights of return or price protection on unsold products held by them. In these instances, the Company recognizes revenue when it ships the product directly to the distributors.

The Company records estimated reductions to revenue under distributor and customer incentive programs, including certain cooperative advertising and marketing promotions and volume-based incentives and special pricing arrangements, at the time the related revenues are recognized. For transactions where the Company reimburses a customer for a portion of the customer's cost to perform specific product advertising or marketing and promotional activities, such amounts are recorded as a reduction of revenue unless they qualify for expense recognition. Shipping and handling costs associated with product sales are included in cost of sales.

Deferred revenue and related product costs were as follows:

Account	December 31, 2011 (in million $)	December 25, 2010 (in million $)
Deferred revenue	202	254
Deferred cost of sales	79	111
Deferred income on shipments to distributors	123	143

Product Financing Arrangements

When the seller is not due for payments from the buyer until the product is "sold through," the channel inventory held by the buyer is essentially collateral for the seller. In this case, we may have a product financing arrangement and not a sale of products. Accounting guidance indicates that a product financing arrangement exists if the following two criteria are met.[3]

1. The arrangement requires the seller to repurchase the product, or processed goods that the product is a component of, at specified prices, and the prices are not subject to change, except for changes due to financing or holding costs.
2. The amount the seller will pay to repurchase the products covers the buyer's purchasing and holding costs, including interest.

The following case illustrates a product financing arrangement.[4]

Fact Set

A company (sponsor) sells a portion of its inventory to another company (the entity through which the financing flows), and in a related transaction agrees to repurchase the inventory. The sponsor arranges for the other entity to acquire a portion of the sponsor's inventory. The other company's sole asset is the transferred inventory that is, in turn, used as collateral for bank financing. The proceeds of bank financing are then remitted to the sponsor.

The debt of the other company is guaranteed by the sponsor. The inventory is stored in a public warehouse during the holding period. The sponsor in connection with the sale (legal title passes to the other company) enters into a financing arrangement under which the following conditions are met.

1. The sponsor agrees to pay all costs of the other company associated with the inventory, including holding and storage costs.
2. The sponsor agrees to pay the other company interest on the purchase price of the inventory equivalent to the interest and fees incurred in connection with the bank financing.
3. The sponsor agrees to repurchase the inventory from the other company at a specified date for the same price originally paid by the other company to purchase the inventory irrespective of changes in market prices during the holding period.
4. The other company agrees not to assign or otherwise encumber the inventory during its ownership period, except to the extent of providing collateral for bank financing.

Analysis

In this product financing arrangement, certain criteria are present, namely (a) the seller is contractually obligated to repurchase the product at a specified price and (b) the seller agrees to pay all holding and financing costs. The sponsor neither records a sale nor removes the inventory from its balance sheet. The sponsor will recognize a liability when the proceeds are received from the other company. Financing and holding costs are accrued by the sponsor as incurred by the other company. Interest costs are separately identified and accounted for by the sponsor.

Customer Return Rights

Product-driven companies routinely offer to their customers return rights. It is important for us to distinguish the generic term "return rights" from what accountants mean when they record return rights. A general right of return, 100% satisfaction guaranteed, is considered a subjective right of return because it may be exercised at will by the customer. Accounting guidance for these types of returns states that if there is significant uncertainty as to whether, or to what extent, the return right will be exercised, then no revenue can be recognized, until the company has reasonable evidence of returns such that it can reliably estimate the amount of returns.[5]

Rights of exchange are also accounted for differently from rights of return. These "like kind" exchanges (same attributes and prices) are not treated as returns and have no effect on the recognition of revenue. The accounting is to recognize the costs of fulfilling the customer's request of exchanging the sold product for a similar (same) product at the time of the original sale.

Return rights granted to customers does call into question whether or not the company's revenue amount is fixed or determinable. Normally, when the product is delivered, if the terms make it clear that the customer has control over the product for his own use, then a sale has occurred. Additionally, provided the company can estimate the actions that customers will take, or not take, an appropriate reserve for returns amount is recorded. This reserve for returns account is deducted from the gross revenue reported by the company when preparing its profit and loss (P&L) statement.

In making the determination that the actions of customers can be estimated and the sale transaction is not an "in substance" consignment, the seller is required to analyze the following accounting criteria.[6]

1. The sales price is fixed or determinable.
2. Payment from customer is not contractually dependent on the buyer's sell through of the product.
3. The buyer has inventory risk of loss, and the loss from theft or damages.
4. The buyer has economic substance apart from the seller. Lack of economic substance on the part of the buyer calls into question whether the buyer is merely acting as an agent for the seller.
5. The seller does not have significant ongoing involvement for future performance relating to resale of the product. In this case, the earnings process is not complete.
6. The amount of the returns can be reasonably and reliably predicted.

When determining an estimate of the amount of expected returns a company will experience for a product or group of products, the company would consider the following.[7] (Note that the following factors are to be interpreted individually and not collectively.)

1. The return period is long. The longer the return period, the more difficult it is to predict the amount of returns.
2. The product is subject to significant external factors, including technological obsolescence and changes in demand.
3. Lack of relevant historical evidence of returns for similar products or products produced on the same product platform. Companies need to have evidence of actions customers would or would not take regarding return behavior.
4. Absence of a volume of homogeneous transactions. It is generally difficult to predict the actions of a customer, but provided a company has sufficient volume of "sales," it has evidence of patterns forming in predicting return behavior.
5. Inventory levels at distributors that are in excess of business norms based on previous purchasing patterns. This is called channel stuffing by the SEC and calls into question the company's ability to predict the amount of returns that will be made by their channel partner.
6. The product is new to the firm. This does infer that you cannot look to similar products when estimating returns.

The aforementioned accounting guidance requires a management cussion about your relationships with channel partners and a data analysis approach to the examination of sales patterns and trends. Note, companies are allowed to analogize to previous generations of products or to new products made in a similar manner to previous versions of the products.

If an estimate of customer returns cannot be made, the seller needs to defer revenue recognition until the earlier of these two: (a) the return period expires or (b) the company can make a reasonable estimate of returns. In addition, if revenue is deferred, no cost of sales and no reduction of inventory can be recorded. Any cash collected would be recorded as a liability.

The following example illustrates accounting for rights of return.

Fact Set

A company sells 200 units of product X at $100 per unit. The inventory cost of each unit is $65. Customers can return the good for up to a 45-day period from the date of sale. The company determines that a reasonable estimate is that 5% of the items will be returned. Also, assume that actual returns were 4%.

Analysis

Assets =	liabilities	+ SE (+revenue) (−expense)

To record the revenue, and the refund liability for possible cash payments

+ Cash + 20,000	+ refund liability + 1,000	+ revenue + 19,000

To record the cost of sales at (200) (65) (95%)

− Inventory − 12,350		− cost of sales + 12,350

To adjust refund liability to actual and record additional revenue

	− Refund liability − 200	+ revenue + 200

To adjust cost of sales and inventory to the actual amounts

− Inventory − 130		− Cost of Sales − 130

Product Warranties

Generally, warranty provisions require the seller to repair or replace the product if it fails to perform as specified contractually. Since these provisions would require the seller to incurr additional costs the sellers would spell out the warranty provisions carefully in the contract. There are two acceptable approaches to accounting for product warranties.

1. Treat the product and the warranty as a multiple-deliverable arrangement (see Chapter 2). Revenue would then be allocated to the two deliverables based on the relative-selling-price method. The revenue allocated to the product would be recognized on delivery and the revenue allocated to the warranty would be recognized over the warranty period.
2. The other acceptable approach is to treat the warranty as part of the product cost and not account for it as a separate revenue deliverable. This approach is the preferred accounting approach when companies include a standard warranty for all buyers of the product. The company recognizes revenue on delivery of the product and then estimates its warranty costs and records the appropriate warranty expense and liability under warranty.

The accounting for separately priced extended warranty and product maintenance contracts differs for the aforementioned treatment of "standard" warranties. Any warranty contract is separately priced if the customer can purchase the product with or without the warranty contract. For example, a customer can purchase an automobile with a standard 4-year, 48,000-mile warranty, can purchase an additional 4-year, 50,000-mile warranty, or both. The pricing of the separately priced warranty is incremental and significant to the BESP of the 4-year, 48,000-mile warranty.

The separately priced extended warranty would be accounted for as a separate unit of accounting, apart from other deliverables in a multiple-element arrangement. The revenue recognition would then be recognized as ratable over the warranty period, or as warranty costs are incurred provided a pattern exists based on historical experience of homogeneous transactions.

The following revenue disclosure by Dell Corporation from their 10-K for 2011 is informative of the accounting for standard and extended warranties offered by the company.

Dell Corporation 10-K for 2011

Warranty liability and deferred extended warranty revenue

Dell records liabilities for its standard limited warranties at the time of sale for the estimated costs that may be incurred. The liability for standard warranties is included in accrued and other current and other noncurrent liabilities on the Consolidated Statements of Financial Position. Revenue from the sale of extended warranties is recognized over the term of the contract or when the service is completed, and the costs associated with these contracts are recognized as incurred. Deferred extended warranty revenue is included in deferred services revenue on the Consolidated Statements of Financial Position. Changes in Dell's liabilities for standard limited warranties and deferred services revenue related to extended warranties are presented in the following tables:

	Fiscal year ended		
	January 28, 2011 ($)	January 29, 2010 ($)	January 30, 2009 ($)
Warranty liability			
Warranty liability at beginning of period	912	1,035	929
Costs accrued for new warranty contracts and changes in estimates for preexisting warranties[a,b]	1,046	987	1,180
Service obligations honored	1,063	1,110	1,074
Warranty liability at end of period	895	912	1,035
Current portion	575	593	721
Noncurrent portion	320	319	314
Warranty liability at end of period	895	912	1,035

	Fiscal year ended		
	January 28, 2011 (in million $)	January 29, 2010 (in million $)	January 30, 2009 (in million $)
Deferred extended warranty revenue			
Deferred extended warranty revenue at beginning of period	5,910	5,587	5,233
Revenue deferred for new extended warranties[b]	3,877	3,481	3,470
Revenue recognized	3,371	3,158	3,116
Deferred extended warranty revenue at end of period	6,416	5,910	5,587
Current portion	2,959	2,906	2,601
Noncurrent portion	3,457	3,004	2,986
Deferred extended warranty revenue at end of period	6,416	5,910	5,587

[a]Changes in cost estimates related to preexisting warranties are aggregated with accruals for new standard warranty contracts. Dell's warranty liability process does not differentiate between estimates made for preexisting warranties and new warranty obligations.
[b]Includes the impact of foreign currency exchange rate fluctuations.

Customer Acceptance Provisions

Customer acceptance provisions generally allow a customer to cancel the sales transaction when the delivered product does not meet the customer's specified criteria. These types of revenue arrangements are generally classified as: (a) acceptance based on seller meeting standard seller specified terms and conditions and (b) acceptance based on customer-specified performance terms and conditions.

In the case of acceptance based on seller-specified criteria, revenue recognition depends on whether the seller has compiled sufficient evidence on its delivered products meeting the specified criteria. If the seller has demonstrated that it can meet its own criteria, then the customer action, which may result in a refund or repair, is treated as a product warranty.

When the customer can specify the performance criteria for a delivered product, the revenue-recognition standard becomes more difficult to apply. These transactions normally involve delivery and installation of equipment in the buyer's location. The problem is that it may be difficult to replicate the buyer's location and the only real way to determine meeting performance specifications is to install the equipment at the client's location.

The standard remains the same: If the seller can reliably demonstrate that the customer-specified performance criteria can be met, the company can recognize revenue or delivery. The company also needs to be able to reliably estimate any additional costs of compliance with the customer-specified performance criteria.

If the company, however, because of the customization is required to deliver under the customer's performance criteria and then cannot conclude prior to delivery that it can reliably meet customer expectations, then the revenue is deferred. The deferral period will last until the customer has "signed off" on the contract indicating customer acceptance.

The following example demonstrates the revenue issues for customer acceptance terms and conditions.[8]

Fact Set

Company E is an equipment manufacturer whose main product is generally sold in a standard model. The contracts for sale of that model provide for customer acceptance to occur after the equipment is received and tested by the customer. The acceptance provisions state that if the equipment does not perform to Company E's published specifications, the customer may return the equipment for a full refund or a replacement unit, or may require Company E to repair the equipment so that it performs up to published specifications. Customer acceptance is indicated by either a formal sign-off by the customer or by the passage of 90 days without a claim under the acceptance provisions. Title to the equipment passes upon delivery to the customer. Company E does not perform any installation or other services on the equipment it sells and tests each piece of equipment against its specifications before shipment. Payment is due under Company E's normal payment terms for that product—30 days after customer acceptance.

Company E enters into an arrangement with a new customer to deliver a version of its standard product modified as necessary to fit into a space of specific dimensions while still meeting all of the published vendor specifications with regard to performance. In addition to the customer acceptance provisions relating to the standard performance specifications, the customer may reject the equipment if it does not conform to the specified dimensions. Company E creates a testing chamber of exactly same dimensions as specified by the customer and makes simple design changes to the product so that it fits into the testing chamber. The equipment still meets all of the standard performance specifications.

Analysis

The contract effectively includes two customer acceptance clauses—one based on a customer-specific criterion and one based on standard performance specifications. For the customer acceptance clause based on the customer-specific criterion, Company E demonstrates that the equipment shipped meets that objective criterion before shipment. As such, there are no uncertainties related to that customer acceptance clause that affect revenue recognition. For the customer acceptance clause based on the standard performance specifications, Company E demonstrates that the equipment shipped meets those specifications before shipment as well. This customer acceptance clause should be evaluated as a warranty obligation. If Company E can reasonably and reliably estimate the amount of warranty obligations, it should recognize revenue upon delivery of the equipment with an appropriate liability for probable warranty obligations (provided the other criteria for recognition are met).

IBM Corporations' revenue arrangements footnote for 2011 is a good summary of revenue-recognition practices for a diversified product and service provider that illustrates the revenue topics we have covered so far.

IBM 10-K 2011

The company recognizes revenue when it is realized or realizable and earned. The company considers revenue realized or realizable and earned when it has persuasive evidence of an arrangement, delivery has occurred, the sales price is fixed or determinable and collectability is reasonably assured. Delivery does not occur until products have been shipped or services have been provided to the client, risk of loss has transferred to the client, and either client acceptance has been obtained, client acceptance provisions have lapsed, or the company has objective evidence that the criteria specified in the client acceptance provisions have been satisfied. The sales price is not considered to be fixed or determinable until all contingencies related to the sale have been resolved.

The company recognizes revenue on sales to solution providers, resellers, and distributors (herein referred to as "resellers"); when the reseller has economic substance apart from the company, credit risk, title and risk of loss to the inventory, the fee to the company is not contingent upon resale or payment by the end user, the company has no further obligations related to bringing about resale or delivery and all other revenue recognition criteria have been met.

The company reduces revenue for estimated client returns, stock rotation, price protection, rebates, and other similar allowances. Revenue is recognized only if these estimates can be reasonably and reliably determined. The company bases its estimates on historical results taking into consideration the type of client, the type of transaction, and the specifics of each arrangement. Payments made under cooperative marketing programs are recognized as an expense only if the company receives from the client an identifiable benefit sufficiently separable from the product sale whose fair value can be reasonably and reliably estimated. If the company does not receive an identifiable benefit sufficiently separable from the product sale whose fair value can be reasonably estimated, such payments are recorded as a reduction of revenue.

Accounting for Sales Incentives Offered to Customers

In order to move product and drive sales, companies often engage in various forms of sales incentives. These may take many forms but the most common are coupons, rebates, discounts on future purchases, and point and loyalty programs. Each of the aforementioned sales incentives will be explained and the accounting illustrated with an emphasis on their impact on revenue recognition.

Coupons and Rebates

Coupons (buy one get one free) and rebates ($30 mail in rebate off the price of a printer) are used by the recipient of the offer in a single transaction. The estimated cost of a coupon or rebate is recognized at the later of the date at which the related sale is recorded by the company or the date at which the sales incentive is offered.

Similar to other revenue-recognition guidance, when the company can reasonably and reliably estimate actions that customers will or won't take, the company can then record the revenue at the time of sale and not at the expiration period of the coupon or rebate offered to customers.[9] The reasonable estimate of redemption of the coupon or rebate made by the company would be recorded as a reduction of revenue. This sales incentive liability account would be subsequently adjusted as evidence of actual redemption rates received by the company and paid out in cash as redemptions occur.

If reasonable estimates of redemption cannot be made (first-time offer, new product, unproven sales channel), then accounting guidance requires that the maximum liability be recorded in the sales incentive liability account. The following factors may impair a company from making a reasonable estimate of redemption of coupons or rebates.[9]

- *The offer period is long.* This makes it difficult to predict response rates.
- *The absence of relevant historical experience.* This would make prediction a guess, not allowed in accounting.
- *The absence of a large volume of homogeneous transactions.* It is generally possible to predict the actions of customers in the aggregate.

The following example illustrates the accounting for coupons.[10]

Fact Set

A manufacturer distributes coupons in a computer magazine offering $300 off the price of Model R computers. The manufacturer will reimburse any retailer for the reduction in the selling price resulting from coupons redeemed by customers on Model R computers. The cost of the Model R computers to the manufacturer is $1,000. The cost of Model R to the retailer is $1,400 (revenue to manufacturer).

Analysis

Assets =	liabilities	+ SE (revenue)

The sales incentive liability, for one transaction, would be recorded at $300 and the sales account would be recorded at $1,100 which is the net amount the manufacturer would receive for the sale to the retailer.

To record the sale and the liability for the sales incentive

+ Cash + 1,400	+ sales incentive + 300	+ revenue + 1,100

To record redemption of the coupon

	− Cash − 300	− sales incentive − 300

Note: The liability for sales incentive would be multiplied by the number of coupons expected to be used, provided the company has historical evidence of homogeneous transactions. To illustrate: assume that the manufacturer sold 2,000 computers at $1,400 to a retail chain and estimated 60% redemption rate of the coupon of Model R computers. Sales were made on cash.

+ Cash + 2,800,000	+ sales incentives + 360,000	+ revenue + 2,440,000

Liability calculation is 2,000(300) (60%)

To illustrate when a company cannot make a reasonable estimate of customer actions, assume that in the entry above the company has to record the maximum liability.

| + Cash + 2,800,000 | + sales incentives + 600,000 | + revenue + 2,200,000 |

A volume rebate may be offered to customers as an incentive to purchase large quantities of manufacturer or retailer output. These incentives normally result in the customer receiving a refund once they have crossed the contractually agreed-upon amount in units. The "cost" of these incentives should be recognized as the customer makes progress in achieving the refund to purchasing products.[11] The preferred account to accrue these "costs" would be the revenue offset account sales returns and allowances. The amount recorded in the offset account would be the company's reasonable estimate of the amount of the rebates. If no reasonable estimate can be made, then the company would record the maximum.

The accounting would be

Assets =	liabilities	+ SE (revenue)
	+ Liability for volume rebate	− sales returns and allowances

Another sales incentive offered is that the company offers a price-protection guarantee on its sales of products. For example, a retailer offers to price match a product and return to the customer the difference on any item that is available for sale in their retail outlets.

This revenue transaction appears to be a multiple-element arrangement, with product sold and the buyer put option back to the company if he purchases the same product for lesser price. However, accounting guidance is to reasonably estimate the "cost" of offering the price-protection option and reduce revenue for the accounting estimate for the price-protection offering. The accounting guidance is also clear that the company needs reasonable evidence of the amount of customers who will take advantage of this contractual provision. Absent evidence of the number of customers who will avail themselves of this option, the company would be required to reduce revenue for all customers who purchase the price-protection item.

Apple Corporations revenue footnote for 2011 is illustrative of their accounting for sales incentives.

Apple Corporation 10-K for **2011**

The Company records reductions to revenue for estimated commitments related to price protection and other customer incentive programs. For transactions involving price protection, the Company recognizes revenue net of the estimated amount to be refunded. For the Company's other customer incentive programs, the estimated cost of these programs is recognized at the later of the date at which the Company has sold the product or the date at which the program is offered. The Company also records reductions to revenue for expected future product returns based on the Company's historical experience. Revenue is recorded net of taxes collected from customers that are remitted to governmental authorities, with the collected taxes recorded as current liabilities until remitted to the relevant government authority.

Discounts on Future Purchases

Chapter 2—Multiple-Element Arrangements—dealt with this topic in some depth. As applied to the purchase of future products, when the discount is incremental and more than insignificant, then the discount represents a separate unit of accounting for the seller. The discount on future purchases offered by the seller is incremental and significant when:

- The discount is incremental when compared to the range of discounts typically offered to customers.
- The discount is significant in the context of the overall consideration to be received from the buyer.

The following illustration provides accounting guidance for accounting for discounts in a multiple-element product arrangement.

Fact Set

A manufacturer sells product X for $120 as well as the right to a discount of 40% on the price Y. The best estimate of selling price of Y is $100. The 18% discount on the total transaction value ($40/ ($120 + $100) is considered significant.

Analysis

Assets =	liabilities	+ SE (revenue)

The overall discount of 18% should be allocated to both products X and Y. So for product X, the allocation of the discount is $120(18%) = $21.60 and for product Y the amount is $100 (18%) = $18. The accounting would be

+ Cash + 120	+ deferred revenue + 21.6	+ revenue + 98.4

To record sale of product X, with deferral for the discount

+ Cash + 60	– deferred revenue – 21.6	+ revenue + 82.6

Point and Loyalty Programs

Awarding points for purchases of the company's products is an attempt by the company to build customer loyalty to their branded products and services. There are a myriad of these types of programs available to the consumer, especially credit card companies and airlines. We will take a fundamental approach to these programs and the subsequent impact on revenue recognition.

The most easily understood programs are those in which the company grants points that are redeemable for the company's products. In this transaction, the company is essentially selling two deliverables, one is the product purchased, the other being the right to future products by redeeming the points earned from purchasing the product. For example, buying an airline ticket enables the customer to travel to his or her destination and after earning sufficient points flying somewhere else for free. The economics of the transaction seem to indicate that this is a multiple-element arrangement (Chapter 2).

This is where the accounting guidance may get confusing. Multiple deliverable revenue arrangements (ASC 605-25) specifically exclude point and loyalty programs when discussing what types of revenue transactions need to apply their accounting guidance. However, companies may elect to apply the separation and allocation guidance for multiple-element arrangements to determine the revenue earned from sales of products that award points to buyers. In that case, the revenue allocated to the point's component of the transaction would be deferred revenue until the points are redeemed.

Companies not electing to account for the revenue transaction as a multiple-element arrangement would accrue the "cost" of awarding free or reduced-price products and services. For example, airlines generally accrue a cost against the revenue for a booked flight, for the expected cost of "free" flight. The difference is that under the accrued cost approach, revenue is reported as gross equal to the price of the ticket sold, with an estimated "cost" of the "free" flight also recorded as an expense.

The following illustrates the revenue recording and reporting for point and loyalty programs.

Fact Set

A company sells a variety of consumer cleaning products. For each dollar of purchases made, the buyer earns one point. These points can be redeemed for any cleaning product the company sells. Assume that buyer's purchases total $100,000, which translates to 100,000 points. Additional points can be purchased on the company's website for $0.24. Products are redeemed which cost the company $15,000.

Analysis

Selling price of cleaning products:	$100,000
Selling price of points (1,000 × 0.24):	$24,000
Total:	$124,000
Arrangement consideration:	$100,000
Allocated to cleaning products: ($100,000/$124,000) ($100,000)	$81,000
Allocated to points (24,000/$100,000) ($100,000)	$19,000
Total:	$100,000

Assets =	liabilities	+ SE (revenue)

To record the revenue and the liability for points awarded

+ Cash + 100,000	+ product liability + 19,000	+ revenue + 81,000

Buyers redeem their points

	− points liability − 19,000	+ revenue + 19,000
− Inventory − 15,000		− cost of sales − 15,000

Accounting for Gift Cards

Companies find gift cards to be very useful in tying customer loyalty to their products and services. In addition, the company gets the cash upfront before delivering the product or service. The revenue, from gift card sales, is then deferred until the customer redeems the gift card and receives the goods or services. Many gift cards carry no expiration date and not everyone who purchases or receives a gift card redeems them. The revenue question is: Can the company, if it is able to reasonably predict the amount of gift card usage, recognize revenue for unused gift cards. Similar to other accounting guidance for recognizing revenue, if a company has sufficient historical evidence of actions its customer will or will not take, then the company can accrue the revenue for unused gift cards for each reporting period.

Apple Corporations' revenue-recognition footnote for deferred revenue is informative as to accounting for gift cards as well as other deferred revenue arrangements.

Apple Corporation 10-K for **2011**

The Company records deferred revenue when it receives payments in advance of the delivery of products or the performance of services. This includes amounts that have been deferred for unspecified and specified software upgrade rights and nonsoftware services that are attached to hardware and software products. The Company sells gift cards redeemable at its retail and online stores, and also sells gift cards redeemable on the iTunes Store for the purchase of digital content and software. The Company records deferred revenue upon the sale of the card, which is relieved upon redemption of the card by the customer. Revenue from Apple-Care service and support contracts is deferred and recognized over the service coverage periods. AppleCare service and support contracts typically include extended phone support, repair services, web-based support resources, and diagnostic tools offered under the Company's standard limited warranty.

The accounting entries involving the recording of selling, redeeming, and estimating unused gift cards are illustrated as follows.

Assets =	liabilities	+ SE (revenue)

To record cash received from gift card sales

+ Cash + xxx	− deferred revenue + xxx	

To record revenue for the redemption of gift card amounts

	− deferred revenue − xxx	+ revenue − xxx

To record revenue for the company's estimate of gift cards that will be unused

	− deferred revenue − xxx	+ revenue − xxx xxx

The following revenue footnote from *Chipotle Mexican Grill*, Inc., for 2011 is instructive accounting for revenue arrangements from gift cards.

Chipotle 10K for 2011

Revenue from restaurant sales is recognized when food and beverage products are sold. The Company reports revenue net of sales and use taxes collected from customers and remitted to governmental taxing authorities.

The Company sells gift cards which do not have an expiration date and it does not deduct non-usage fees from outstanding gift card balances. The Company recognizes revenue from gift cards when: (i) the gift card is redeemed by the customer or (ii) the Company determines the likelihood of the gift card being redeemed by the customer is remote (gift card breakage) and there is not a legal obligation to remit the unredeemed gift cards to the relevant jurisdiction. The determination of the gift card breakage rate is based upon Company-specific historical redemption patterns. The Company has determined that 5% of gift card sales will not be redeemed and will be retained by the Company. Gift card breakage is recognized in revenue as the gift cards are used on a pro rata basis over a six month period beginning at the date of the gift card sale. Gift card breakage is included in total revenue in the consolidated statement of income. Breakage recognized during the years ended December 31, 2011, 2010 and 2009 was $1,524, $1,188 and $878, respectively.

Gross Versus Net Revenue Reporting

The last topic for this chapter is concerned with the determination of whether the seller should report revenue at the gross (principal) amount or at the net (agent). For example, normally when a real-estate "agent" sells property, the company would record the revenue as net. The net in this case refers to the commission received from either the buyer or the seller and not at the value of the property sold, which would be gross revenue reporting.

The determination of whether the seller should report revenue gross or net is a matter of professional judgment based on the sales arrangement. Accounting guidance, in this area, lists a set of factors for when it is appropriate to record the revenue at the sales prices and when it is appropriate to record revenue at the amount of "fee" received.[12]

The following eight indicators may support reporting gross revenue.

1. **The company is the primary obligor in the arrangement**
   If the selling company is responsible for fulfillment of a customer order that is a strong indicator that the entity has the risks and rewards of a principal in the transactions and should record the revenue at the gross amount based on the amount billed to the customer.

2. **The company has general inventory risk—before customer order is placed or upon customer return**
   General inventory risk is a strong indicator that an entity has risks and rewards as a principal in the transaction and, therefore, that it should record revenue gross based on the amount billed to the customer. General inventory risk exists if a company takes title to a product

before that product is ordered by a customer or will take title to the product if it is returned by the customer and the customer has a right of return.

3. **The entity has latitude in establishing price**

   If a company has the right to establish the selling price with a customer for the product or service, that fact may indicate that the company has risks and rewards of a principal in the transaction and that it should record revenue gross based on the amount billed to the customer.

4. **The company changes the product or performs part of the service**

   If a company physically changes the product (beyond its packaging) or performs part of the service ordered by a customer, that fact may indicate that the entity is primarily responsible for fulfillment and that it should record revenue gross based on the amount billed to the customer. This indicator is based on the "seller" adding value to the product and changing the selling price, not from the perspective of marketing skills, marketing channels, or its distribution system.

5. **The company has discretion in supplier selection**

   If an entity has multiple suppliers for a product or service ordered by a customer and discretion to select the supplier that will provide the product or service ordered by a customer, that fact may indicate that the entity is primarily responsible for fulfillment and that it should record revenue gross based on the amount billed to the customer.

6. **The company is involved in the determination of product or service specifications**

   If an entity must determine the nature, type, characteristics, or specifications of the product or service ordered by the customer, that fact may indicate that the entity is primarily responsible for fulfillment and that it should record revenue gross based on the amount billed to a customer.

7. **The entity has physical loss inventory risk—after customer order or during shipping**

   Physical loss inventory risk exists if title to the product is transferred to a company at the shipping point and is transferred from that entity to the customer upon delivery. Physical loss inventory risk also exists if an entity takes title to the product after a customer order has been received but before the product has been transferred to a carrier for shipment. This indicator may provide some evidence, albeit less persuasive than general inventory risk, that an entity should record revenue gross based on the amount billed to the customer.

8. The entity has credit risk

Credit risk exists if an entity is responsible for collecting the sales price from a customer but must pay the amount owed to a supplier after the supplier performs, regardless of whether the sales price is fully collected. This criterion provides some evidence, though not by itself compelling, that the seller is the principal and would record the revenue at the gross amount. The following three indicators may support reporting net revenue.

1. The entity's supplier is the primary obligor in the arrangement

Whether a supplier or an entity is responsible for providing the product or service desired by a customer is a strong indicator of the company's role in the transaction. If a supplier (and not the selling company) is responsible for fulfillment, including the acceptability of the products or services ordered or purchased by a customer, that fact may indicate that the entity does not have risks and rewards as principal in the transaction and that it should record revenue net based on the amount retained (i.e., the amount billed to the customer less the amount paid to a supplier).

2. The amount the entity earns is fixed

If a company earns a fixed dollar amount per customer transaction regardless of the amount billed to a customer or if it earns a stated percentage of the amount billed to a customer, that fact may indicate that the company is an agent of the supplier and should record revenue net based on the amount retained.

3. The supplier has credit risk

If credit risk exists (i.e., the sales price has not been fully collected prior to delivering the product or service) but that credit risk is assumed by a supplier, that fact may indicate that the company is an agent of the supplier and, therefore, the entity should record revenue net based on the amount retained.

Apple Corporations' revenue-recognition footnote for 2011 is illustrative of the company's interpretation of the aforementioned accounting guidance for revenue reporting for gross and net transactions.

Apple Corporation 10-K for 2011

For the sale of most third-party products, the Company recognizes revenue based on the gross amount billed to customers because the Company establishes its own pricing for such products, retains related inventory risk for physical products, is the primary obligor to the customer, and assumes the credit risk for amounts billed to its customers. For third-party applications sold through the App Store and Mac App Store and certain digital content sold through the iTunes Store, the Company does not determine the selling price of the products and is not the primary obligor to the customer. Therefore, the Company accounts for such sales on a net basis by recognizing in net sales only the commission it retains from each sale. The portion of the gross amount billed to customers that is remitted by the Company to third-party app developers and certain digital content owners is not reflected in the Company's Consolidated Statements of Operations.

The following illustrations demonstrate the judgment required in applying the accounting guidance for recording revenue gross (principle) or net (agent).[13]

Fact Set

Company A facilitates the sale of home furnishing products. Each product marketed has a unique supplier and that supplier is identified in product catalogs distributed to customers. Company A maintains no inventories of products in advance of customer orders. Company A takes title to the products ordered by customers at the point of shipment from suppliers. Title is passed to the customer upon delivery. The gross amount owed by a customer is charged to the customer's credit card prior to shipment and Company A is the merchant of record. Company A is responsible for collecting the credit card charges and must remit amounts owed to suppliers regardless of whether that collection occurs. Suppliers set product selling prices. Company A retains a fixed percentage of the sales price and remits the balance to the supplier. Written information provided to customers during marketing and included in the terms of sales contracts states the following.

Company A manages ordering, shipping, and billing processes to help you purchase home furnishing products. Company A does not buy, sell, manufacture, or design the products. When you use Company A, you are purchasing the products from the suppliers. Company A has no control over the quality or safety of the products listed. Orders will not be binding on Company A or the suppliers until the applicable supplier accepts them. Company A will process your requests for order changes, cancellations, returns, and refunds with the applicable supplier. All order changes, cancellations, returns, or refunds are governed by the supplier's policies, and you agree to pay additional shipment costs or restocking charges imposed by the supplier. You agree to deal directly with the supplier regarding warranty issues. Company A will not be liable for loss, damage, or penalty resulting from delivery delays or delivery failures due to any cause beyond reasonable control.

Analysis

Based on an evaluation of the circumstances, some of the indicators point toward gross reporting, while other indicators point toward net reporting. Entity A concludes that revenues should be reported net in this example. Although indicators of gross reporting exist for physical loss inventory risk (during shipping) and credit risk (for collecting amounts charged to credit cards), those indicators are not sufficient to overcome the stronger indicators that revenues should be reported net, including that both:

1. The supplier, not the entity, is the primary obligor.
2. The amount earned by the entity is a fixed percentage of the total amount billed to the customer.

Fact Set

A reseller of office furniture receives an order for a large quantity of desks with unique specifications. The reseller and the customer develop the specifications for the desks and negotiate the selling price for the desks. The reseller is responsible for selecting the supplier. The reseller contracts with a supplier to manufacture the desks communicates the specifications and arranges to have the supplier deliver the desks directly to the customer. Title to the desks will pass directly from the supplier to the customer upon delivery. (The reseller never holds title to the desks.) The reseller is responsible for collecting the sales price from the customer and is obligated to pay the supplier when the desks are delivered, regardless of whether the sales price has been collected. The reseller extends 30-day payment terms to the customer after perform-ing a credit evaluation. The reseller's profit is based on the difference between the sales price negotiated with the customer and the price charged by the selected manufacturer. The order contract between the reseller and the customer requires the customer to seek remedies for defects from the supplier under its warranty. The reseller is responsible for customer claims resulting from errors in specifications.

Analysis

After applying the indicators, the reseller concludes that revenue from the transaction should be reported based on the gross amount billed to the customer. The fact pattern does not clearly point to either the supplier or the reseller as the primary obligor to the cus-tomer. The reseller has complete latitude in negotiating the selling price for the desks and selecting a supplier among alternatives, and it earns a variable amount in the transaction equal to the differ-ence between the selling price negotiated with the customer and the amount to be paid to the supplier, pointing to gross reporting. Finally, the reseller has credit risk from financing amounts billed to customers as accounts receivable, which is a weaker indicator that revenue should be reported gross.

The revenue footnote from FedEx Corporation for 2011 is a good example of how companies apply the gross versus net revenue accounting guidance.

FedEx 10-K for 2011

We recognize revenue upon delivery of shipments for our transpor-tation businesses and upon completion of services for our business services, logistics, and trade services businesses. Transportation services are provided with the use of employees and independent contractors. FedEx is the principal to the transaction for these services and revenue from these transactions is recognized on a gross basis (with the exception of FedEx SmartPost as described below). Costs associated with independent contractor settlements are recognized as incurred and included in the caption "Purchased transportation" in the accompanying consolidated statements of income. For shipments in transit, revenue is recorded based on the percentage of service completed at the balance sheet date. Estimates for future billing adjustments to revenue and accounts receivable are recognized at the time of shipment for money-back service guarantees and billing corrections. Delivery costs are accrued as incurred.

Our contract logistics, global trade services, and certain transportation businesses, such as FedEx SmartPost, engage in some transactions wherein they act as agents. Revenue from these transactions is recorded on a net basis. Net revenue includes billings to customers less third-party charges, including transportation or handling costs, fees, commissions, and taxes and duties.

Certain of our revenue-producing transactions are subject to taxes, such as sales tax, assessed by governmental authorities. We present these revenues net of tax.

CHAPTER 4

Service Revenue

About This Chapter

Revenue from services performed should be recognized when the seller has performed his promised obligations under the contract and the seller has a right to receive consideration from the buyer. For services, revenue is generally earned as the services are being performed—Proportional Performance model—or when the services have been completed—Completed Performance model. The difficulty in accounting for revenue transactions for services performed is that there is a paucity of accounting guidance to aid the company in making a determination as adherence to the general principles of revenue recognition: earned and realizable.

The key factor regarding the analysis of service-based revenue arrangements is in making the determination of the pattern of service delivery or performance. Many service contracts are of a long-term nature, which will require of the company to be able to assert that as they are rendering their services to the buyer, the buyer is receiving value as evidenced by the customer transferring consideration (cash) to the seller.

Since there is very little direct guidance for recording revenue for service contracts, there has been developed what is called "reasoning by analogy" to other nonrelated guidance for service transactions. This chapter will equip you with the reasoning skill to use the relevant accounting guidance for revenue transactions resulting from service transactions.

Performance Models

The Completed Performance model is generally used when we deliver products to customers. The analogy of revenue recognition on delivery can be made to services, when the service consists of performing a single act. For example, you visit a financial planner who charges by the hour.

Each hour of the planner's time with you is revenue to the planner. Note that, whether they would use the Proportional Performance model, say billing increments of 15 minutes, or the Completed Performance model, 1 hour, you arrive at the same amount of revenue.

To extend the example, let's say you are the customer; and you contract with the financial planner for delivery in 3 months' time a comprehensive financial plan. Payment is due on delivery of the financial plan. In this case, even though the seller has numerous activities to perform before delivering the financial plan, it is likely that revenue recognition would be deferred until final delivery. Note that even if the seller would require a 50% payment up-front of the agreed-upon price, the seller would still defer revenue until the financial plan is delivered to the customer.

Performance of Services Involves Multiple Activities

Performing a service in which the seller processes transactions for the buyer would normally use the Proportional Performance model to recognize revenue as each discreet service is performed. In Chapter 2 on multiple-element arrangements, one of the examples used was a company providing payroll-processing services over a 3-year period (36 months). In that case, accounting guidance looks at the service revenue arrangement as 36 separate deliverables. As each one is "delivered" to the buyer, the company would recognize revenue. The principle here is that value is passing to the buyer as each "service deliverable" is performed. Generally, for any transaction that is repetitive either for contractually agreed-upon number of services performed or there is a billing event each time the seller renders the service for the buyer, we analogize to the model for multiple-element arrangements and treat each occurrence as a deliverable.

There are, however, circumstances in which the buyer does not receive the value of the purchase until the last act is performed by the seller. For example, in our previous financial planning scenario in which the seller gets paid when the plan is delivered, the seller may perform the following activities:

- Interview with the buyer to determine risk profile and financial goals.
- Fact-gathering phase for financial solutions appropriate for the client.

- Scenario planning given resources available or planned.
- Final report incorporating best-available advice.

In this example, since the final act of delivering the report is the "value-added" aspect of the arrangement, revenue recognition would occur when the report is delivered. Another example would be a commercial broker that leases office space. There are a number of activities that need to occur prior to the broker leasing the space to the buyer (lessee). However, until the buyer contractually agrees to lease office space, no revenue could be recognized by the seller (broker). The company's determination of whether to use the Proportional Performance model or the Completed Performance model will depend on the facts and circumstances of each revenue arrangement. The following guidance is offered as a template in assisting companies in determining if the last "deliverable" is when value passes to the buyer and the Completed Performance model is preferable in recognizing revenue.[1]

1. If the seller fails to perform the final act, the customer would need to "start over," rather than just pick up where the original seller left off. If the activities being performed by the seller add value to the buyer, then the buyer should not have to re-perform activities already performed by the seller.
2. Payment terms indicate that no payment is due until the final act is performed.
   When no payment is due until the final "deliverable" and that has been contractually agreed to, it would seem to indicate that value passes to the buyer when the seller performs the final activity.
3. The final act is significantly different from the other activities performed by the seller.
   This arrangement may involve the activities performed that result in the final activity, which were performed to enable the seller to perform the final "value-added" act for the buyer.
4. The contractual arrangement specifies the final act and leaves other activities to the discretion of the seller.
   If the acts performed leading up to the final act are not discussed with the seller and are not part of the contractual arrangement, this may indicate that they are unimportant to the buyer.

5. There is significant uncertainty as to whether the seller can complete all the activities in the arrangement.

When the seller is uncertain in his ability to perform the final activity that completes the arrangement, then the seller would not have reliable evidence of his ability to complete the arrangement.

The following illustration demonstrates the application of the aforementioned guidance.[2]

Fact Set

Company M performs claims processing and medical billing services for health-care providers. In this role, Company M is responsible for preparing and submitting claims to third-party payers, tracking outstanding billings, and collecting amounts billed. Company M's fee is a fixed percentage (e.g., 5%) of the amount collected. If no collections are made, no fee is due to Company M. Company M has historical evidence indicating that the third-party payers pay 85% of the billings submitted with no further effort by Company M.

Analysis

Company M must wait until collections occur before recognizing revenue. Despite the fact that Company M estimates that it will not need to put forth any further efforts in 85% of the billings, the fact remains that the final act—collecting the receivables—is of such significance that revenue should not be recognized until it is completed. The importance of collection, as compared to sending the bills and the other acts Company M performs, is evidenced by the fact that payment is not due until collection occurs.

Proportional Performance Model

Companies are concerned with two aspects of the revenue contract when recognizing revenue in a service transaction that delivers services over time and is comprised of more than one activity. First, the company needs to determine the value-creating activities for the buyer that is supplied by the seller. These factors may consist of the following (adapted from ARM, service rev, pages 197–198):

1. Activity performed by the seller is not specifically identified in the contract.

   The lack of specifically stating an activity in a contract makes it less likely that it is value added for the buyer.

2. The activity relates to building the seller's service capacity or training its employees to be able to accomplish the task.

   Activities performed to be able to perform the requested service for the buyer are not "value added" for the buyer.

3. The activity is administrative in nature.

   Administrative activities are indirect "value-added" activities for the buyer.

4. The customer would not be aware that the activity was performed.

   Activities that the buyer perceives as adding value are generally visible to the buyer.

Second, the seller needs to determine how these acts are performed for the buyer. Service transactions differ in the patterns of services that are provided to customers. For example, services can be provided in which there are a specified number of similar activities or a specified number of nonsimilar activities. The recognition of revenue then depends on how the services are delivered and when value is passing to the buyer.

When the delivery of services is indicated by a *specified number of similar activities*, then revenue should be recognized as each service "deliverable" is provided by the seller. The reasoning is that each service activity (processing bimonthly payroll) is determined to be a separate deliverable or separate unit of accounting. (See Chapter 2—Multiple-Element Arrangements.) In accounting for these transactions, the revenue recorded from performing the discrete activity is not influenced by the costs incurred to deliver the service to the buyer. For example, the service provider may need to provide additional training and technical support in the early years of the contract in order to provide the requisite level of service to the customer. Service revenue is not a cost-driven revenue system. When value for performing an activity (deliverable) is transferred to the buyer, revenue is recognized.

Similar to product revenue guidance, companies that can reasonably estimate actions their customers would or would not take are allowed to take that evidence into account when determining the pattern of revenue to be recognized. For example, a payment-processing firm is responsible for processing payments received from customers who are paying car loans. The loan term is 5 years. The company has historical evidence that 40% of the loans are paid off in 4 years. In that case, the company can use their evidence of early prepayment and recognize 40% of the revenue over the 4-year term.

Service providers who deliver a *specified number of dissimilar activities* would like the guidance of multiple-element arrangements (Chapter 2— Multiple-Element Arrangements). For example, a general contractor is awarded a bid to replace windows, install siding, and replace the roof on a residential house. In this situation, we have three deliverables that would be recognized as revenue as each deliverable is completed. The revenue allocation to the three deliverables, provided they have a stand-alone value, would be done using the relative-selling-price method.

When the service provider provides dissimilar acts that do not provide a stand-alone value to the buyer, the seller would recognize revenue on a reasonable basis of the contractual term. The following illustrates the revenue-recognition alternatives when discrete activities are performed by the seller, but do not provide a stand-alone value to the buyer.

Fact Set

An accounting company (Accounting) accepts an audit engagement from a manufacturing company [Manufacturing]). The contractual period is from March 16, 2012, to March 15, 2013. The activities to be performed by Accounting consist of performing the following:

1. Risk-assessment procedures in order to determine the appropriate evidence that needs to be gathered from testing the company's internal controls over financial transactions and evidence from determining the correctness of the company's account balances in order to form an opinion as to the fairness of Manufacturing's financial statements.

2. Tests of the company's internal controls over financial reporting to determine whether Manufacturer's assertion that his controls are effective in producing reliable financial reporting of the
   company's financial statements.
3. Tests of the account balances to assure compliance with Generally Accepted Accounting Principles (GAAP) and the amounts
   recorded are not materially misstated.
4. Issue the audit report of fairness in all material respects of the
   company's financial statements.

Analysis

The "value added" to the buyer of the accounting service occurs
when the audit report is issued. The activities listed earlier indicate not providing a stand-alone value to the buyer because, if
Accounting is taken off the engagement prior to completion,
then the next accounting firm hired would, in fact, start over
with the aforementioned activities. Accounting would recognize
revenue in this case, generally, when the discrete activities listed
earlier have been performed. Another revenue-recognition pattern for Accounting could be based on periodic meetings with
Manufacturing to discuss the progress of the audit. Each meeting then may represent a significant event in determining the
progress made to the final activity, which is the issuance of the
audit report.

Service contracts can also take the form of a "retainer" agreement.
In this arrangement, the seller agrees to provide an unspecified number
of similar acts for a period. For example, customer contracts with seller
to provide snow-removal services for the winter season for their business
for a fixed sum. The predictability of weather would be very difficult; so
revenue-recognition guidance would be that the fixed sum is apportioned
ratably over the contract term.

The last service revenue pattern occurs when the seller offers services
over an indeterminate length of time for the buyer. For example, car
repair businesses may offer a lifetime guarantee on the vehicle while in the
customer's ownership, for a fee, on certain parts installed on automobiles.

In this case, provided the company has historical evidence of the life of the automobile repaired, the company would recognize revenue over the expected useful life of the automobile for that owner. Note if the company cannot make reasonable estimates of customer actions (sell or trade-in the car, thereby avoiding the warranty), they would recognize revenue when performance obligation has been satisfied or is no longer applicable to the company.

The following revenue-recognition footnotes from *American Airlines Corporation and Six Flags Entertainment Corporation* illustrate how those companies have applied accounting guidance for service revenue transactions.

American Airlines Corporation 10-K for 2011

Passenger ticket sales are initially recorded as a component of Air traffic liability. Revenue derived from ticket sales is recognized at the time service is provided. However, due to various factors, including the complex pricing structure and interline agreements throughout the industry, certain amounts are recognized in revenue using estimates regarding both the timing of the revenue recognition and the amount of revenue to be recognized, including breakage. These estimates are generally based upon the evaluation of historical trends, including the use of regression analysis and other methods to model the outcome of future events based on the Company's historical experience, and are recorded at the scheduled time of departure.

Six Flags Entertainment Corporation 10-K for 2011

We recognize revenue upon admission into our parks, provision of our services, or when products are delivered to our customer. For season pass and other multiuse admissions, we recognize a pro rata portion of the revenue as the guest attends our parks. Revenues are presented net of sales taxes collected from our guests and remitted to government taxing authorities in the accompanying consolidated statements of operations. Deferred income at December 31, 2011 primarily reflects advanced sales of 2012 season passes.

Accounting for Fees Received in Advance from Customers

Customers who want to access certain service provider's offerings may be required to pay a portion of the total value of the service as an up-front fee. The question for the company is how much, if any, of the advance fee should be recognized as revenue. Generally, an up-front fee provides the customer with access to services over a period of time. For example, Health Clubs frequently require a member to pay an up-front fee as well as an ongoing fee in order for the member to access their services. In this case, the up-front fee would be deferred revenue and apportioned as revenue over the length of the contractual term.

In other instances, a service provider may assess an up-front fee as compensation to the provider for costs incurred in being able to offer the service. Revenue recognition would generally be ratably earned over the contractual period as the customer uses the service. For example, Internet Portal Acme requires a $100 payment up-front for the right to access their databases for a period of 2 years. The up-front payment is intended to compensate the company for customizing its database for its customers. Provided the customization is not a multiple-element transaction, the company would recognize revenue for the up-front fee ratably over the contractual period.

Service providers assess an up-front fee for providing initiation and or installation services that meet the requirements for being accounted for as a multiple-element arrangement. When the initiation, installation, or both services have (a) stand-alone value and the (b) performance of providing the service is substantially in control of the seller, then the service provider has met the requirements that the initiation, installation, or both are a separate unit of accounting for purposes of recognizing revenue (Chapter 2—Multiple-Element Arrangements).

The following examples illustrate the accounting guidance for revenue recognition when service providers receive an up-front fee.[3]

Fact Set

Companies may negotiate arrangements pursuant to which they may receive nonrefundable fees upon entering into arrangements or on certain specified dates. The fees may ostensibly be received for conveyance of a license or other intangible right or for delivery of particular products or services. Various business factors may influence how the registrant and customer structure the payment terms. For example, in exchange for a greater up-front fee for an intangible right, the company may be willing to receive lower unit prices for related products to be delivered in the future. In some circumstances, the right, product, or service conveyed in conjunction with the nonrefundable fee has no utility to the purchaser separate and independent of the company's performance of the other elements of the arrangement. Therefore, in the absence of the company's continuing involvement under the arrangement, the customer would not have paid the fee. The following examples demonstrate accounting guidance for revenue arrangements when companies receive an up-front fee.

1. *Selling a membership*: A company sells a lifetime membership in a health club. After paying a nonrefundable "initiation fee," the customer is permitted to use the health club indefinitely, as long as the customer also pays an additional usage fee each month. The monthly usage fees collected from all customers are adequate to cover the operating costs of the health club.

2. *Signing a contract*: A company in the biotechnology industry agrees to provide research and development activities for a customer for a specified term. The customer needs to use certain technology owned by the registrant for use in the research and development activities. The technology is not sold or licensed separately without the research and development activities. Under the terms of the arrangement, the customer is required to pay a nonrefundable "technology access fee" in addition to periodic payments for research and development activities over the term of the contract.

3. *Activating services—monthly usage fee*: A company requires a customer to pay a nonrefundable "activation fee" when entering into an arrangement to provide telecommunications services. The terms of the arrangement require the customer to pay a

monthly usage fee that is adequate to recover the registrant's operating costs. The costs incurred to activate the telecommunications service are nominal.

4. *Activating services—1-year fee*: A company charges users a fee for nonexclusive access to its website that contains proprietary databases. The fee allows access to the website for a 1-year period. After the customer is provided with an identification number and trained in the use of the database, there are no incremental costs that will be incurred in serving this customer.

5. *Activating services—advertising services*: A company charges a fee to users for advertising a product for sale or auction on certain pages of its website. The company agrees to maintain the listing for a period of time. The cost of maintaining the advertisement on the website for the stated period is minimal.

6. *Initial setup service*: A company charges a fee for hosting another company's website for 1 year. The arrangement does not involve exclusive use of any of the hosting company's servers or other equipment. Almost all of the projected costs to be incurred will be incurred in the initial loading of information on the host company's internet server and setting up appropriate links and network connections.

Analysis

Accounting guidance requires that the company consider the specific facts and circumstances for each revenue transaction in order to determine the appropriate accounting for nonrefundable, up-front fees. Unless the up-front fee is in exchange for products delivered or services performed that represent the culmination of a separate earnings process (represents a separate unit of accounting in a multiple-element arrangement), the deferral of revenue is appropriate over the contractual service period.

In the six examples described earlier, the accounting guidance would not view the activities completed by the companies (selling the membership, signing the contract, enrolling the customer, activating telecommunications services, or providing initial setup services) as separate units of accounting in determining the timing of revenue recognition.

The terms, conditions, and amounts of these fees typically are negotiated in conjunction with the pricing of all the elements of the arrangement, and the customer would ascribe a significantly lower, and perhaps no, value to elements ostensibly associated with the up-front fee in the absence of the registrant's performance of other contract elements. The fact that the registrants do not sell the initial rights, products, or services separately supports the accounting guidance that the fees paid can be accounted for as a separate unit of accounting for revenue-recognition purposes.

Accounting guidance indicates that the customers are purchasing the ongoing rights, products, or services being provided through the registrants' continuing involvement. Furthermore, accounting guidance would indicate that the earnings process is completed by performing under the terms of the arrangements, not simply by originating a revenue-generating arrangement.

While the incurrence of nominal up-front costs helps make it clear that there is not a separate earnings event in the *activating services* examples mentioned earlier, incurrence of substantive costs, such as in the *initial setup service* example mentioned earlier, does not necessarily indicate that there is a separate earnings event. Whether there is a separate earnings event should be evaluated on a case-by-case basis. Accounting guidance indicates that unless there is a separate unit of accounting using the revenue guidance for multiple-element arrangements, revenue should be recorded ratably over the contractual term.

Supply or service transactions may involve the charge of a nonrefundable initial fee with subsequent periodic payments for future products or services. The initial fees may, in substance, be wholly or partly an advance payment for future products or services. In the aforementioned examples, the ongoing rights or services being provided or products being delivered are essential to the customers receiving the expected benefit of the up-front payment.

Therefore, the up-front fee and the continuing performance obligation related to the services to be provided or products to be delivered are assessed as an integrated package. In such circumstances, accounting guidance would make the determination that up-front fees, even if nonrefundable, are earned as the products, services, or both are delivered, performed, or both over the term of the arrangement or the expected period of performance and generally should be deferred and recognized systematically over the periods that the fees are earned.

The revenue-recognition period should extend beyond the initial contractual period if the relationship with the customer is expected to extend beyond the initial term and the customer continues to benefit from the payment of the up-front fee (e.g., if subsequent renewals are priced at a bargain to the initial up-front fee).

A systematic method would be on a straight-line basis, unless evidence suggests that revenue is earned or obligations are fulfilled in a different pattern, in which case that pattern should be followed.

To further illustrate the accounting guidance when receiving an up-front fee, we refer to *Wal-Mart's* revenue-recognition footnote concerning their selling of memberships to *Sam's Club*.

The Company recognizes membership fee revenue both in the United States and internationally over the term of the membership, which is 12 months. The following table summarizes membership fee activity for fiscal 2012, 2011, and 2010.

(Amounts in millions)	Fiscal years ended January 31,		
	2012	2011	2010
Deferred membership fee revenue, beginning of year	$542	$532	$541
Cash received from members	1,111	1,074	1,048
Membership fee revenue recognized	(1,094)	(1,064)	(1,057)
Deferred membership fee revenue, end of year	$ 559	$ 542	$ 532

Membership fee revenue is included in membership and other income in the Company's Consolidated Statements of Income. The deferred membership fee is included in accrued liabilities in the Company's Consolidated Balance Sheets.

Direct and Incremental Costs Incurred for Service Delivery

Accounting for costs incurred for service providers would typically be recognized under the Proportional Performance model as the services are being performed. In service revenue that is recognized when the service is complete, accounting guidance permits deferral of costs of providing the service until the revenue is recognized.

The majority of costs to be incurred for services transactions are those costs that are directly related to providing the services to customers. There is little disagreement among accountants as to the "correct" method of recording these costs. As the direct and incremental (costs that would not be otherwise incurred absent the revenue arrangement) costs are incurred, the company records them as expenses to be charged against the resultant revenue.

Accounting for other direct costs that are incurred by companies to procure customer contracts is a difficult area for companies to navigate in applying the appropriate accounting guidance. The problem is that accounting guidance for expense recognition is specific to a particular type of transaction or particular to a specific industry. For example, the accounting principles have guidance for cost of sale, employee compensation, advertising, environmental costs, and specific expense guidance for insurance companies, media companies, software companies, as well as a host of other industries.

Other costs that are incurred in procuring a customer contract may include *customer acquisition costs, costs incurred in negotiating the contract, and paying sales commissions to employees, as well as costs related to setup and installation costs* that are not a separate unit of accounting in the revenue arrangement. The accounting question to answer is: Should these costs be capitalized and then expensed against the revenue when the revenue is earned, or should they be expensed as incurred?

The accounting policy decision to either capitalize and "match" against the revenue when earned or to expense as incurred will depend on the following:

1. *Capitalize and amortize over the revenue stream.* Managements desire to attribute costs incurred prior to performing services for the customer against the revenue when earned, thereby "smoothing" the earnings stream from the revenue arrangement. Companies would choose this option if their intent is to more readily determine the income earned per accounting period by more closely matching the costs incurred against the revenue earned.

2. *Expense as incurred.* Companies would choose this alternative when their intent for a revenue arrangement is to report the income earned by only charging costs incurred during the revenue process against the revenue earned. In this case, management believes that the costs of procuring the customer contracts are an ongoing portion of the business.

Capitalizing *customer acquisition costs* as well as other costs incurred before contract performance begins are to be analyzed using the model for loan solicitation and origination costs.[4] Costs eligible to be capitalized are determined using the following model:

1. Incremental direct costs incurred with third parties
2. Internal direct costs related to the origination activities

Companies would substitute contract-acquisition costs for loan solicitation and origination costs when applying the model for their company. Wages and salaries incurred would be limited to the amount of work done on origination. Salesperson commissions can also be capitalized to the extent that they perform both customer acquisition and administrative work to finalize the contract.

Setup and installation costs that are eligible to be capitalized cover the time period between when the revenue arrangement is signed and before services are performed for the customer. These costs would include those of the activities that would be performed by the service provider in order to be able to provide services to the buyer. The accounting guidance permits capitalization of incremental direct setup costs after the contract is obtained.[5]

The following guidance is indicative of generally accepted accounting practice regarding accounting for setup costs in revenue arrangements.[6]

Fact Set

Company A provides its customers with activity tracking or similar services (e.g., tracking of property tax payment activity, sending delinquency letters on overdue accounts, etc.) for a 10-year period. Company A requires customers to prepay for all the services for the term specified in the arrangement. The ongoing services to be provided are generally automated after the initial customer setup. At the outset of the arrangement, Company A performs setup procedures to facilitate delivery of its ongoing services to the customers. Such procedures consist primarily of establishing the necessary records and files in Company A's preexisting computer systems in order to provide the services. Once the initial customer setup activities are complete, Company A provides its services in accordance with the arrangement. Company A is not required to refund any portion of the fee if the customer terminates the services or does not utilize all of the services to which it is entitled. However, Company A is required to provide a refund if Company A terminates the arrangement early. Assume that this arrangement qualifies as a single unit of accounting.

Are the initial customer setup costs incurred by Company A eligible capitalization?

Analysis

Accounting guidance would be that the incremental direct costs incurred related to the acquisition or origination of a customer contract in a transaction that results in the deferral of revenue may be either expensed as incurred or accounted for and shall be deferred and charged to expense in proportion to the revenue recognized.

Fact Set[7]

A satellite TV company (Satellite) sells receivers and satellite dishes and provides satellite television programming to customers. Satellite enters into a transaction with Customer M (M) where M purchases a satellite dish and receiver and signs a contract to receive 1 year of satellite programming. M installs the satellite dish and receiver itself. Amounts to be paid by M include a $50 up-front, nonrefundable fee, and $30 per month for the duration of the contract. If the customer cancels the contract early, a $200 cancellation fee is due to Satellite. The costs incurred by Satellite include:

- $150 related to its purchase of the receiver and satellite dish from a third party;
- $15 of origination costs (allocated employee costs for 1.25 hours spent by an employee to perform a credit check and process paperwork);
- $25 of setup costs (allocated employee costs for 1.5 hours spent activating the receiver and satellite dish to receive Satellite's signals);
- $100 commission paid to an internal employee dedicated solely to selling activities.

Satellite has concluded that it should not separate the sale of the receiver and satellite dish from the satellite programming services. Furthermore, Satellite has concluded that the up-front fee should be deferred over a period of 3 years (expected customer relationship period) using the straight-line method.

Analysis

Each of the costs listed earlier should be evaluated as follows:

- Receiver and satellite dish—The costs of the receiver and satellite dish are incremental direct costs paid to a third party. They are eligible for deferral.

- Performing credit check and processing paperwork—The amounts related to an internal employee performing a credit check and processing paperwork are direct internal origination costs. These costs are generally eligible for deferral:

1. Activating receiver and satellite dish—The amount related to an internal employee activating the receiver and satellite dish to receive Satellite's signals represents direct payroll-related costs incurred in connection with setup activities. These costs are generally eligible for deferral.

- Commission—The commission paid to an internal employee dedicated solely to selling activities is likely eligible for deferral as long as the commission is paid only for successful efforts—that is, only when a contract is generated.

Based on this evaluation, the total amount of potentially capitalizable costs is $290. As discussed earlier, the receiver and dish costs would be required to be capitalized. Satellite could elect to capitalize the other costs or expense them as incurred. In addition, Satellite might conclude that capitalizing only some of the setup, commission, origination, or all costs would provide the most transparent presentation to investors and could likely justify a policy reflecting that judgment. For example, Satellite might decide to capitalize only the incremental costs of a new contract, which would cause Satellite to expense the setup and origination costs, but capitalize the sales commissions.

Computer Sciences Corporations' revenue disclosure for capitalizing setup costs and their subsequent amortization is instructive in accounting for costs incurred to directly generate revenue.

Computer Sciences Corp. Form 10-K for 2010

Outsourcing Contract Costs

Costs on outsourcing contracts, including costs incurred for bid and proposal activities, are generally expensed as incurred. However, certain costs incurred upon initiation of an outsourcing contract are deferred and expensed over the contract life. These costs represent incremental external costs or certain specific internal costs that are directly related to the contract acquisition or transition activities. Such capitalized costs can be separated into two principal categories: contract acquisition costs and transition/setup costs. The primary types of costs that may be capitalized include labor and related fringe benefits, subcontractor costs, travel costs, and asset premiums.

The first principal category, contract acquisition costs, consists mainly of due diligence activities after competitive selection as well as premiums paid. Premiums are amounts paid to clients in excess of the fair market value of acquired assets. Fixed assets acquired in connection with outsourcing transactions are capitalized at fair value and depreciated consistent with fixed asset policies described above. Premiums are capitalized as outsourcing contract costs and amortized over the contract life. The amortization of outsourcing contract cost premiums is accounted for as a reduction in revenue. The second principal category of capitalized outsourcing costs is transition/setup costs. Such costs are primarily associated with installation of systems and processes and are amortized over the contract life.

In the event indications exist that an outsourcing contract cost balance related to a particular contract may be impaired, undiscounted estimated cash flows of the contract are projected over its remaining term and compared to the associated asset group including the unamortized outsourcing contract cost balance. If the projected cash flows are not adequate to recover the unamortized cost balance of the asset group, the balance would be adjusted based on the contract's fair value in the period such a determination is made. The primary indicator used to determine when impairment testing should be performed is when a contract is materially underperforming, or is expected to materially underperform in the future, as compared to the original bid model or subsequent annual budgets.

Refunds and Rights of Return

Service providers generally allow their customers to cancel, partially or in full, if the service does not meet contractual expectations. Similar to product sales, revenue recognition may have to be deferred for the company until customer acceptance is received or the refund or return rights period has lapsed.

Customer rights of return generally are categorized as a subjective refund right (satisfaction guaranteed), customer acceptance provisions on the seller meeting their specified performance criteria, and seller meeting the buyer's specified criteria. The timing of the recording of revenue depends on the type of refund or return that is offered to the customer in the revenue arrangement.

The promise by the seller to the buyer that the service provides a "warranty" of 100% satisfaction is in substance a cancellation right for the buyer. The accounting guidance for product returns is clearly stated in allowing revenue recognition when the right of return exists provided the companies have historical evidence of estimating returns for similar products. Unfortunately, this guidance does not apply to service arrangements (ASC 605-15-25).

Accounting practice for service arrangements has developed two responses to the lack of accounting guidance as it regards revenue recognition when the right of return or cancellation rights exists for the buyer.

1. Companies can use the model of estimating returns for product companies. This results in revenue being recognized by the service provider as the company performs the required service, with an accrual of the estimate of refunds or returns that they expect to make to customers. The key is to have historical evidence of similar transactions that allows the company to provide a reasonable estimate. The accrual would be recorded in sales returns and allowances.

2. Other companies look to accounting guidance for financial liabilities because they believe that the right of return or refund is in essence a financial promise to pay. In that case, since the "liability" is only extinguished when it is paid or the return period expires, no amount that would be estimated to be subject to return can be recognized as revenue until the "liability" is paid or it lapses (ASC 405-20-40).

If the company elects to apply the accounting model for estimating returns or refunds the company by reference to the product revenue model, then it must determine whether the requirements have been met. The requirements to be satisfied are as follows (see Chapter 3—Product Revenue—for an extensive discussion on revenue when the right of return exists):

1. Price to the buyer is fixed or determinable.
2. The buyer has economic substance apart from the buyer.
3. The seller does not have significant ongoing involvement for future performance relating to the refundable service.
4. The amount of returns and refunds can by reasonably estimated.

The following examples illustrate the accounting guidance for service companies offered a right of refund to customers.

Fact Set

Exotic Travel Company offers a membership for $2,000 per year that entitles the customer to two vacations per year (airfare not included). Exotic offers a pro rata or full refund depending on the vacations taken. ($1,000 refund if customer cancels membership after taking one vacation.) Exotic sold 100 memberships in 2012. Five customers elected for the full refund and 12 customers elected the refund after they had taken one vacation.

1. Company analogizes that the refund is a financial liability in which revenue is not recognized until the liability (refund) has expired.

Financial statement impact is demonstrated as follows:

Asset	= liabilities	+ SE (revenue)

Payment is received

Asset	= liabilities	+ SE (revenue)
+ Cash + 200,000	+ refund liability +200,000	

Cash is refunded to five members

– Cash – 10,000	– refund liability – 10,000	

Cash is returned to the 12 customers for the partial refund

– Cash – 12,000	– refund liability – 12,000	

Revenue is recognized on remaining memberships after expiration of refund offer

	– refund liability – 78,000	+ revenue + 78,000

2. Exotic Travel Company follows a policy of recording revenue for membership sales when they occur provided refund estimates can be made with a reasonable degree of certainty. Assume that vacations are taken equally by members over 12 months. Also assume that the company estimated the refund rate at 10% for partial refunds and 5% for full refunds.

   Financial statement impacts are demonstrated as follows:

Asset	= liabilities	+ SE (revenue)

Payments are received from members and Exotic accrues for the refund liability

+ Cash + 200,000	+ deferred revenue + 180,000	+ refund liability + 20,000

Exotic recognizes revenue ratably for the first month of the year

	– deferred revenue – 15,000	+ revenue +15,000

Note: this entry is made 11 more times under the Proportional Performance model

Exotic records the refunds paid for cancellations

– Cash – 20,000	– refund liability – 20,000	

Customer acceptance terms that specify a refund or return based on standard seller specifications would generally give the customer the right to cancel the service or receive a refund if the service does not deliver on its promises. For example, Sales Company sells 1,000 customer leads to Real

Estate Company. Sales Company guarantees Real Estate that the leads will generate a 20% conversion rate resulting in sales of property. For each percentage point less than 20%, Sales will refund to Real Estate 5% of the price paid. In this case, provided the seller has previously demonstrated the ability to meet his own specified criteria, the company would record the guarantee as a warranty.

Customer acceptance provisions that are specified by the customer would generally be the most difficult in determining whether the seller has fulfilled his requirements until the service period is completed. One of the reasons for this is that as each service activity is performed, the customer would need to accept that activity as complete prior to performing the next activity. In addition, service providers would generally be allowed to continue working if customer specifications are not met for an activity. These factors would seem to indicate that value, and therefore revenue recognition, is passed to the buyer when the project is complete.

However, if the service provider's offerings are specialized for particular clients, then the company may have sufficient historical evidence that it can meet its service activities (obligations) and then the Proportional Performance model may be appropriate. It is important to note that revenue-recognition guidance applies to each revenue arrangement. Therefore, each customer contract must be evaluated, which may result in different patterns of revenue recognition for different contracts with buyers.

Service Warranties

Service arrangements that involve the product installation (mechanics, building contractors) generally are packaged with a service warranty. The warranty is usually "paid" by re-performing the service contractual agreed to with the customer. Warranty provisions need to be evaluated by the seller in making a determination as the obligations it is incurring with customer in fulfilling the revenue arrangements.

When service providers warrant to customers performance specifications that go beyond their own standard warranties, it may be difficult to reasonably estimate the activities necessary to meet their obligations in the contract. When this is the case, revenue is deferred until the performance specifications are met. For example, Machinery warrants that its equipment will meet customer tolerances of precision of 99.5% for a period of 24 months. Failure to achieve that standard in any 1 month requires that Machinery retrofit the equipment to achieve the 99.5 tolerance level for the next month's production. Depending upon its historical experience with meeting that tolerance requirement for the specific class of customer, Machinery may have to defer the recognition of revenue monthly as it meets the customer specifications.

Companies have two choices in accounting for warranty contracts. One, treat the service arrangement as a multiple-element arrangement; the service initially performed being one deliverable and the warranty period as the second deliverable. The amount of consideration allocated to the warranty would be recognized over the contractual period. The second approach is to treat the warranty as an integral part of providing the service. This method does not treat the warranty "deliverable" as a separate unit of accounting. The estimated costs of these standard warranties would be added to cost of sales when the revenue from the arrangement is recognized.

Service providers will also warrant performance over extended periods of time. If these extended warranty contracts are separately priced and offer additional services over the "standard" warranty, then the amount received would be deferred and recognized as revenue ratably over the extended warranty period. For example, Car Repair Company offers a standard warranty for 1 year on all parts and services performed. In addition, customers can purchase an additional warranty that covers all parts and services for an additional 2 years. This arrangement consists of two separate units of accounting: (a) service performed initially and standard warranty and (b) the separately priced extended warranty. The separate unit of accounting for the initial service performed and the standard warranty would be accounted for as one deliverable with an appropriate allocation to the cost of the standard warranty obligation. The separately priced extended warranty would be recognized as revenue when the service(s) are performed ratably over time.

The revenue disclosure for Midas Corporation's 10-K for 2011 offers useful accounting guidance regarding the revenue treatment of service warranties.

Midas, Inc., Form 10-K for 2011

Recognition of Warranty Costs

Customers are provided a written warranty from MDS on certain Midas products purchased from Midas shops in North America, namely brake friction, mufflers, shocks, and struts. The warranty will be honored at any Midas shop in North America and is valid for the lifetime of the vehicle, but is voided if the vehicle is sold. The Company maintains a warranty accrual to cover the estimated future liability associated with outstanding warranties. The Company determines the estimated value of outstanding warranty claims based on: (1) an estimate of the percentage of all warranted products sold and registered in prior periods at retail that are likely to be redeemed; and (2) an estimate of the cost of redemption of each future warranty claim on a current cost basis. These estimates are computed using actual historical registration and redemption data as well as actual cost information on current redemptions.

Annual warranty activity is summarized as follows (in millions):

Fiscal Year	2010	2009	2008
Accrued warranty expense at beginning of period	$13.3	$16.5	$24.8
Warranty benefit, net	(0.3)	(0.3)	(2.7)
Changes in foreign currency exchange rate	0.1	0.5	(1.1)
Warranty credit issued to franchisees (warranty claims paid)	(2.3)	(3.4)	(4.5)
Accrued warranty expense at end of period	10.8	13.3	16.5
Less current portion	1.7	2.0	2.4
Accrued warranty—noncurrent	$9.1	$11.3	$14.1

Warranty expense (benefit) is included in operating costs and expenses in the statements of operations. A portion of warranty expense incurred is also paid as claims within the same fiscal year. Warranty expense was reduced by $0.3 million, $0.6 million, and $3.4 million in fiscal 2010, 2009 and 2008, respectively, due to changes in estimated warranty redemptions.

As of January 1, 2008, the Company changed how the Midas warranty obligations are funded in the United States. From June 2003 to December 2007, product royalties received from the Company's preferred supply chain vendors were recorded as revenue and substantially offset the cost of warranty claims. Beginning in fiscal 2008, the Midas warranty program in the United States is funded directly by Midas franchisees. The franchisees are charged a fee for each warranted product sold to customers. The fee is charged when the warranty is registered with the Company. The fee billed to franchisees is deferred and is recognized as revenue when the actual warranty is redeemed and included in warranty expense. This fee is intended to cover the Company's cost of the new warranty program, thus revenues under this program will match expenses and the new warranty program will have no impact on the results of operations. In connection with this change, beginning in 2008 Midas system franchisees in the United States started receiving rebates on their purchases from the Company's preferred supply chain vendors and MDS no longer receives product royalties on Midas franchisee purchases in the United States. Because the Company's U.S. supply chain partners are responsible for the warranty of parts during the first 12 months, MDS did not begin to record revenues or expenses under the new program until fiscal 2009.

As of July 1, 2009, the Company changed how the Midas warranty obligations are funded in Canada to match the U.S. program. As a result, beginning in July 2009 Midas system franchisees in Canada started receiving rebates on their purchases from the Company's preferred supply chain vendors and MDS no longer receives product royalties on Midas franchisee purchases in Canada. Because the Company's Canadian supply chain partners are responsible for the warranty of parts during the first 12 months, MDS did not begin to record revenues or expenses under the new Canadian program until fiscal 2010.

Annual activity for the deferred warranty obligation related to this new program is summarized as follows (in millions):

Fiscal Year	2010	2009	2008
Deferred warranty obligation at beginning of period	$5.3	$3.0	—
Warranty fees charged to franchisees and company-operated shops	2.8	2.8	3.0
Warranty credits to company-operated shops	(0.1)	—	—
Warranty credits to franchisees (recognized as revenue and expense)	(1.2)	(0.5)	—
Deferred warranty obligation at end of period	$6.8	$5.3	$3.0

CHAPTER 5

Revenue from Contracts with Customers

About This Chapter

The Financial Accounting Standards Board (FASB) in conjunction with the International Accounting Standards Board (IASB) have been diligently working on a major revision to accounting guidance for revenue recognition for over 5 years. The result of their efforts has been the issuance of an exposure draft and a reexposure draft that was issued based on practitioner comments on their dissatisfaction to the original exposure draft. The FASB and the IASB continue to deliberate with a final standard expected in the first quarter of 2013.

Given the critical importance of revenue recognition for companies and the relative certainty that a new standard will be issued next year, this chapter will focus on the key elements of the "new" revenue model. Revenue from contracts with customers will leverage the accounting guidance for multiple-element transactions and apply that revenue model to each revenue transaction with a customer. There will be, however, substantial differences for recognizing revenue and its related costs using present accounting guidance and the application of the "new" revenue model.

The other crucial aspect of the new revenue standard is that the revised revenue-recognition guidance will be applied retrospectively. The anticipated application date of the new standard will be for fiscal years ending 2015. Since accounting standards generally require three income statements and two balance sheets, companies would need to start rearranging their revenue data systems to produce pro forma results for 2013.

This chapter is designed as a comprehensive review of Revenue from Contracts with Customers. The intent of the chapter is to equip the accounting practitioner with a firm understanding of the new revenue-recognition guidance, so that when the actual standard is released in 2013, the company, with minor alterations, will have a head start on recognizing any changes to their current revenue-recognition accounting policies.

The new revenue model has a five-step framework that companies will apply to each of their contracts with customers. These foundational principles are:

1. Identify contracts with customers
2. Identify the separate performance obligations (deliverables) in the contract
3. Determine the transaction price
4. Allocate the transaction price to the separate performance obligations
5. Recognize revenue when the company satisfies each performance obligation.

This chapter will now cover each of the aforementioned elements of the framework.

Identify the Contract with the Customer

The first step in applying the framework is to identify the contract with the customer (similar analysis in determining evidence of a revenue arrangement). Accounting guidance will include all contracts that create enforceable rights for the seller to receive cash or other assets for the delivery of products or services or right to use assets to the buyer will apply the framework. The contract may be written, oral, or implied by the company's business practices. In determining whether a contract exists, companies will apply the following criteria:[1]

1. The contract has commercial substance (i.e., the risk, timing, or amount of the entity's future cash flows is expected to change as a result of the contract).
2. The parties to the contract have approved the contract (in writing, orally, or in accordance with other customary business practices) and are committed to perform their respective obligations.

3. The entity can identify each party's rights regarding the goods or services to be transferred.
4. The entity can identify the payment terms for the goods or services to be transferred.

Note that the requirement under existing accounting guidance to have a fixed or determinable amount in order to recognize revenue is not contemplated in the new model. Instead, any transfer of goods and services to the buyer under the arrangements "contractual" terms would create enforceable claims for the seller against the buyer to receive cash or other assets. The new guidance establishes that if a company can estimate the transaction price to be paid by the buyer (even if not stated in the contract), then it has satisfied the "fixed or determinable" criteria for the recognition of revenue.

The following illustrates guidance for nonpriced obligations. The examples include a product, a service, and changes when we have one performance obligation.

Fact Set

General Contractor enters into a fixed-price contract with Office Company to construct an office building. During the building process, Office requested additional structural improvements different from the original design. General prepared a change order for the scope of the additional work to be performed and both parties agreed to the change order. However, the change to the final price would be agreed to at completion of the building.

Analysis

The change order contract has commercial substance and each party can determine their obligations under the contract. As long as there are enforceable rights under the contract and General has sufficient evidence such that it is able to estimate the transaction price, then the change order contract qualifies for revenue recognition as they are performing the work.

In a revenue arrangement when the seller and buyer agree to modify the existing contract, companies will then need to determine if the "amended" contract now qualifies as a separate performance obligation (separate unit of accounting). The new revenue model would require a company to account for the modification as a separate performance obligation if the modified contract results in one of the following (paragraph 21):

1. The incremental goods and services are distinct. The exposure draft defines distinct as (a) the company regularly sells the item separately or (b) the customer can benefit from the good or service either on its own or together with other resources that are readily available to the customer.
2. The company's ability to receive the stand-alone selling price of the promised incremental goods and services.

The accounting guidance for "deliverables" that are not considered distinct will differ from current accounting practice for multiple-element arrangements. Transfer of the buyer of multiple "deliverables" that are not distinct would require the seller to account for the transfers as a single unit of accounting if both of the following conditions are met:[2]

1. The goods or services in the bundle are highly interrelated and transferring them to the customer requires that the entity also provide a significant service of integrating the goods or services into the combined item(s) for which the customer has contracted.
2. The bundle of goods or services is significantly modified or customized to fulfill the contract.

The examples that follow illustrate the accounting for modifications to existing contracts in determining revenue recognition. The examples are adapted from Proposed Accounting Standards Update (Revised): Revenue Recognition (Topic 605).

Fact Set

An entity promises to sell *120 products* to a customer for $12,000 ($100 per product). The products are transferred to the customer at various points in time over a 6-month period. The contract is modified after 60 products have been transferred, and the entity promises to deliver an additional *30 products* for an additional $2,850 or $95 per product. The pricing for the additional products reflects the stand-alone selling price of the products at the time of the contract modification. In addition, the additional products are distinct from the original products because the entity regularly sells the products separately.

Analysis

Therefore, the contract modification for the additional *30 products* is, in effect, a new and separate contract for future products that does not affect the accounting for the existing contract. If the pricing for the additional products did not reflect the stand-alone selling price of the additional products, the entity would allocate the modified transaction price (less the amounts allocated to products transferred at or before the date of the modification) to all remaining products to be transferred. Consequently, the amount recognized as revenue for each of the remaining products would be a blended price of $98.33 ([($100 × 60 products not yet transferred under original contract) + ($95 × 30 products to be transferred under the contract modification)] ÷ 90 remaining products) per product.

Fact Set

An entity enters into a 3-year *services contract*. The customer promises to pay $100,000 at the beginning of each year. The stand-alone selling price of the services at contract inception is $100,000 per year. At the end of the second year, the contract is modified and the fee for the third year of services is reduced to $80,000. In addition, the customer agrees to pay an additional $200,000 to extend the contract for 3 additional years (i.e., 4 years remain after the modification). The stand-alone selling price of the services at the beginning of the third year is $80,000 per year. The entity's stand-alone selling price multiplied by the number of years is deemed to be an appropriate estimate of the stand-alone selling price of the multiyear contract (i.e., the standalone selling price is 4 years × $80,000 per year = $320,000).

Analysis

At the date of modification, the entity evaluates the *remaining services* to be provided and concludes that they are distinct. However, the amount of remaining consideration to be paid ($280,000) does not reflect the standalone selling price of the services to be provided ($320,000). Hence, the entity would reallocate the remaining consideration of $280,000 to the remaining services to be provided and would recognize revenue of $70,000 per year ($280,000 ÷ 4 years) as the *services are provided.*

Fact Set

An entity enters into a contract to construct a house for a customer, which is considered to be a single performance obligation. That is, the goods and services in the bundle are *highly interrelated* and providing them to the customer requires the entity also to provide a significant service of integrating the goods or services into the combined item (i.e., the house) for which the customer has contracted. In addition, the goods or services are *significantly modified and customized to* fulfill the contract. At inception, the entity expects the following:

Transaction price:	$1,000,000
Expected costs:	800,000
Expected profit (20%):	$200,000

By the end of the first year, the entity has satisfied 50% of its performance obligation on the basis of costs incurred ($400,000) relative to total expected costs ($800,000). Hence, the cumulative revenue and costs recognized for the first year are as follows:

Revenue:	$500,000
Costs:	400,000
Gross profit:	$100,000

At the beginning of the second year, the parties to the contract agree to change the floor plan of the house. As a result, the contract revenue and expected costs increase by $100,000 and $75,000, respectively.

Analysis

The entity concludes that the remaining goods and services to be provided under the modified contract are not distinct because the entity provides a significant service of integrating the highly interrelated goods and services into the combined item (the house) for which the customer has contracted. In addition, providing the house requires the entity to significantly modify the promised goods and services.

Consequently, the entity accounts for the contract modification as if it were part of the original contract. The entity updates its measure of progress and estimates that it has satisfied 45.7% of its performance obligation ($400,000 actual costs incurred ÷ $875,000 total expected costs). In addition, the entity would recognize an additional revenue of $2,700 (45.7% complete × $1,100,000 modified transaction price – $500,000 revenue recognized to date).

Identify the Separate Performance Obligations in the Contract

This is the critical step in the framework because the number of performance obligations will determine the number of separate units of accounting in determining the amount and timing of revenue recognition. A performance obligation is a promise made by the seller to transfer a product or service to the buyer. Performance obligations are relatively similar to deliverables in multiple-element arrangements. However, as noted earlier in identifying the contract phase of applying the framework, there are instances when delivering a combination of goods and services will result in one performance obligation.

When we have separate units of accounting in revenue arrangements, companies will generally use the Completed Performance model in recognizing revenue for products. Companies that provide service performance obligations will generally use the Proportional Performance model in recognizing revenue. When companies are selling integrated solutions that combine goods and services and they conclude that there is only one performance obligation under the revenue arrangement, then revenue will be recognized proportionately over the contract.

Performance obligations may include the following (paragraph 26):

1. Goods produced by an entity for sale (e.g., inventory of a manufacturer).
2. Goods purchased by an entity for resale (e.g., merchandise of a retailer).
3. Providing a service of arranging another party to transfer goods or services to the customer (e.g., acting as an agent of another party)
4. Standing ready to provide goods or services (e.g., when-and-if-available software products).
5. Constructing, manufacturing, or developing an asset on behalf of a customer.
6. Granting licenses or rights to use intangible assets.
7. Granting options to purchase additional goods or services (when those options provide the customer with a material or economically significant right).

The performance obligations listed here are similar to determining separate units of accounting in a multiple-element arrangement. Understanding the framework of determining deliverables will generally serve you very well in determining performance obligations.

The following examples illustrate this critical phase of the new revenue model.

Fact Set

An entity licenses customer relationship management software to a customer. In addition, the entity promises to provide consulting services to significantly customize the software to the customer's information technology environment for a total consideration of $600,000.

The entity is providing a significant service of *integrating the goods and services* (the license and the consulting services) into the combined item for which the customer has contracted. In addition, the software is significantly customized by the entity in accordance with the specifications negotiated with the customer.

Analysis

In this case, the entity would account for the license and consulting services together as *one performance obligation*. Revenue for that performance obligation would be recognized over time by selecting an appropriate measure of progress toward complete satisfaction of the performance obligation.

Fact Set

Company A, a specialty construction firm, enters into a contract with a municipality to design, construct, and operate a tolled roadway beneath a body of water. The municipality solicited bids from multiple firms on all three phases of the project—design, construction, and operation.

The design and construction of the tunnel and roadway involves multiple goods and services from architectural consultation and engineering through procurement and installation of all of the materials. Several of these goods and services *could be considered separate performance obligations* because Company A frequently sells the services, such as architectural consulting and engineering services, as well as stand-alone construction services based on third-party design, separately.

Given the highly complex nature of this project, Company A will be required to continually alter the design of the tunnel and roadway during construction as well as continually assess the propriety of the materials initially selected for the project.

Analysis

Company A concludes that the design and construction phases are highly dependent on one another (i.e., the two phases are highly interrelated). Company A also determines that significant customization and modification of the design and construction services are required in order to fulfill the performance obligation under the contract. Therefore, Company A concludes that the design and construction services will be bundled and accounted for as one performance obligation. However, Company A concludes that the operation phase of the arrangement is not highly interrelated with the design and builds services, and that operation phase is a separate performance obligation.

Fact Set

Now assume that Company A concludes that the design of the tunnel and roadway is expected to be completed prior to the construction, and that it will not require any significant modification during the construction phase. Although the construction is dependent on the design, the design is not dependent on the construction. Furthermore, the design services and construction services are fulfilled with separate resources.

Analysis

Based on the weight of the evidence, Company A concludes that the design and construction phases are not highly interrelated. As the proposed model requires both criteria to be met (highly interrelated and significant customization or modification) to treat goods and services within a bundle as a single performance obligation, Company A concludes that the design and construction phases, each would be accounted for as separate performance obligations.

Additionally, Company A concludes that the subsequent operation of the tolled roadway would not be bundled with the design or construction projects. The subsequent operating activities are not highly interrelated with the design and construction phases. Therefore, Company A would treat the subsequent operation of the toll road as a separate performance obligation.

Fact Set

Company A is in the business of outfitting office space with telephone and computer networking infrastructure and computer hardware. The entity has recently contracted with three customers to provide outfitting services at three different levels. The following table illustrates the goods and services under contract with each customer:

Services to be Provided	Customer 1	Customer 2	Customer 3
Custom design	X		
Transfer of the equipment	X	X	X
Installation	X	X	
Employee training	X		

Entity A must evaluate whether the goods or services under each contract are highly interrelated, whether transferring them to the customer requires a significant integration service, and whether the bundle of goods or services is significantly modified or customized to fulfill the contract.

Analysis

Customer 1—This arrangement is with a large international customer that has complex requirements for its networking infrastructure. As a result, Entity A concludes that providing a full solution from design of the systems through a customized installation also requires the entity to manage the integration of each of the components. Therefore, Entity A would account for the design to installation project as a single performance obligation— the delivery of a customized, fully implemented telephone and IT network. Because employee training is not a component that is integrated in providing the network to the customer, Entity A would analyze that performance obligation for separability from the other components using the criteria described earlier.

Customer 2—This arrangement is with a customer that does not require Entity A to develop the design of the networking infrastructure. However, the project will require a significant integration effort by Entity A to get all of the components to work together. Therefore, Entity A will have to determine if, in order to satisfy the requirements of the arrangement, they are either significantly modifying or customizing the equipment as part of the installation. If significant modification or customization is required, then the entire arrangement would be treated as a single performance obligation. If not, the entity may conclude that the equipment can be accounted for as a separate performance obligation from the installation efforts.

Customer 3—Entity A is providing goods only, which includes delivery to the site. It would account for the individual goods separately.

Revenue contracts frequently embed provisions that give the customer the option to purchase additional products or services. These sales incentives vary from offering free products or services (points and loyalty programs) to discounts on future purchases of products and services. In Chapter 2—Multiple-Element Arrangements—if the discount or other sales incentive offered to customers was incremental and significant to the buyer in comparison with the seller's other customers, then the sales incentive would generally be accounted for as a separate deliverable.

The proposed revenue model substitutes the words "material right" for incremental and significant. The meaning of material in the new revenue model is interpreted to be similar to the meanings given to incremental and significant when separating deliverables in multiple-element arrangements using existing accounting guidance.

The following illustrates the recommended guidance when accounting for a volume discount.

Fact Set

A company enters into a contract with a customer to sell Product A for $100 per unit. If the customer purchases more than 1,000 units of Product A in a calendar year, the price per unit is retroactively reduced to $90 per unit. The company's experience is predictive of the amount of consideration to which the entity will be entitled.

For the first quarter ended March 31, the entity sells 90 units of Product A to the customer, and the entity estimates that the customer's purchases will not exceed the 1,000 unit's threshold required for the volume discount in the calendar year.

Analysis

The entity recognizes revenue of $9,000 (90 units × $100 per unit) for the period ended March 31. The entity is reasonably assured to be entitled to that amount.

In June, the entity's customer acquires another company. As a result, the entity estimates that the customer's purchases will exceed the 1,000 unit's threshold for the calendar year. For the second quarter ended June 30, the entity sells an additional 500 units of Product A to the customer. Hence, the entity recognizes a revenue of $44,100 for the period ended June 30. That amount equals $45,000 for the sale of 500 units (500 units × $90 per unit) less $900 (90 units × $10 price reduction) for the reduction of revenue relating to units sold for the quarter ended March 31. The entity is reasonably assured to be entitled to that amount.

Determine the Transaction Price

The transaction price is the amount of consideration expected to be received by the seller from transferred products and services to the buyer. When sellers are making this determination, they will assume that the products and services promised in the contract will be delivered and the contract will not be cancelled, renewed, or modified (paragraph 51). In determining the transaction price, companies will need to perform an analysis of the following components of price in arriving at the amount of revenue expected to be earned and then allocated to the performance obligations. The four components are:[3]

1. Variable consideration
2. The time value of money
3. Noncash consideration
4. Consideration payable to a customer.

Variable consideration consists of the incentives or inducements that companies have in contracts to motivate buyers to do business with them. They include, but are not limited to, discounts, rebates, refunds, penalties, price concessions, and other similar marketing tactics to get customers to buy your products and services.

When estimating variable consideration in order to determine the transaction price companies will use in allocating consideration to performance obligations, companies will use either the "expected-value" approach or the "most-likely-amount" approach. The expected-value approach assigns probabilities to outcomes and then sums them to arrive at an amount. Note that the actual amount of revenue recorded will not be the expected value since it is a sum of determining probabilistic outcomes and then applying them to an amount. The revenue amount to be recorded will be a different amount because it is normally a binary decision by the buyer; exercise the "option" on the particular sales incentive offered or do not exercise. Developing a most-likely estimate is the company's expectation that it will "earn" the revenue or it will not.

For example, if the company is 80% certain that it will earn a performance bonus of $400,000 based on evidence from a large group of similar projects, then the company would accrue the entire $400,000 as revenue as it performs under the contract. Compare that approach with using the expected-value approach. Let's assume we assign the same 80% probability for achieving the bonus and then assign a 0% chance of not earning the bonus. The company would then accrue $360,000 ($400,000 × 80% + 400,000 × 20%) as record as the revenue is earned.

This stage of the framework is a significant change from existing accounting guidance for multiple-element arrangements. As discussed in Chapter 2, companies are limited to allocating revenue to delivered performance obligations that are not contingent on the performance of future performance obligations. The guidance here is the reasonably assured consideration to be received.

The following illustrates the change in accounting guidance (E&Y).

Fact Set

A company operates outsourced call centers for retail and manufacturing companies. It is compensated through fixed minimum amounts plus variable amounts based on average customer wait times. Entity A negotiates a new 3-year contract with a customer it has been serving for the past 3 years. The contract states that the fixed amounts payable for annual services are $12 million per year and $10 per call for calls in excess of 1.2 million. The company also is able to earn semiannual bonus payments of $700,000 if the average customer wait time is less than 4 minutes.

The company determines that the call-center service for 1.2 million calls annually is the only performance obligation in the arrangement. That is, the option to obtain services on additional calls, because it is priced at the same rate per call as the 1.2 million calls, is not an option that provides the customer a material right. Furthermore, based on historical experience, the company does not expect the volume of calls to exceed 1.2 million calls annually.

Analysis

To estimate the total transaction price, the company would consider all reasonably available information, including its past performance on similar contracts. Based on that information, the company expects the average wait time to be less than 4 minutes throughout the year. Therefore, the entity estimates the transaction price as $13,400,000 ($12,000,000 + ($700,000 × 2)) in each year. The company would account for each year as a separate performance obligation and would recognize revenue based on the proportion of calls completed to the total number of calls expected up to 1.2 million calls. In the first year, the company determines that it is reasonably assured to be entitled to the full estimated transaction price; thus, it would recognize as revenue $11 ($13,200,000/1,200,000) per call as the service is provided. Note that if the company expected the volume of calls to exceed 1.2 million calls annually, it would have to include those calls (and the expected consideration) in the total transaction price so that the expected incremental consideration from the calls in excess of 1.2 million is allocated across all expected calls.

Under current accounting guidance, the amount considered fixed or determinable would include only the fixed minimums until the uncertainty about the bonus payments is resolved. Therefore, the entity would record $6,000,000/2 over the first 6 months and at the end of the period would recognize the $700,000 bonus. This results in less revenue recorded in the first quarter due to the uncertainty about the bonus payment.

Revenue arrangements that are long term (over 1 year) often create situations in which the company is financing the buyer, payment occurs after the products and services are delivered, or the customer pays in advance, that is, the customer is providing financing for the company. When a revenue arrangement contains a financing component that is significant, then the company must adjust the transaction price to reflect the price that would have been paid if the buyer paid cash when the products or services were delivered or performed.

When the customer payment and the transfer of products or services exceeds 1 year, then the company is not required to take into account the financing component of the revenue arrangement.

The following example illustrates accounting for a financing component.

Fact Set

An entity enters into a contract to sell Product A and Product B for an up-front cash payment of $150,000. Product A will be delivered in 2 years and Product B will be delivered in 5 years. The entity allocates the $150,000 to Products A and B on a relative stand-alone selling price basis as follows:

	Stand-alone selling prices ($)	Percent allocated	Allocated amounts ($)
Product A	40,000	25	37,500
Product B	120,000	75	112,500
Total	160,000		150,000

The entity uses a financing rate of 6%, which is the entity's incremental borrowing rate.

Analysis

The following demonstrates how an entity would account for the effects of the time value of money for a revenue transaction.

Asset	= liabilities	+ SE

1. Recognize the contract liability for the $150,000 payment at contract inception.

+ Cash + 150,000	+ Contract liability + 150,000	

2. During the 2 years from contract inception until the transfer of Product A, recognize the interest expense on $150,000 at 6% for 2 years.

	+ Contract liability + 18,540	Interest expense − 18,540

($18,540 = $150,000 contract liability × (1.0622 − 1)

3. Recognize revenue for the transfer of Product A.

	− Contract liability − 42,135	+ revenue + 42,135

$42,135 = $37,500 initial allocation to Product A + $4,635, which is Product A's portion (25%) of the $18,540 interest for the first 2 years of the contract.

4. Recognize the interest expense for 3 years on the remaining contract liability of $126,405.

	+ Contract liability + 24,145	− Interest expense − 24,145

$126,405 = $150,000 initial contract liability + $18,540 interest for 2 years - $42,135 derecognized from the transfer of Product A.

$24,145 = $126,405 contract liability balance after 2 years ×
(1.0633 – 1).

5. Recognize revenue for the transfer of Product B.

	– Contract liability – 150,550	+ revenue + 150,550

$150,550 = $126,405 contract liability balance after 2 years +
$24,145 interest for 3 years.

Consideration received from the customer may be in the form or products, services, or other noncash assets. Present accounting guidance refers to revenue arrangement as a nonmonetary transaction. Existing guidance looks to the fair value (selling price) of the products, services, or other noncash assets transferred in valuing the products, services, or other noncash assets received. The proposed revenue model will be the opposite. The company will arrive at a fair value of the products, services, or other noncash assets received under the revenue arrangement and record that amount as revenue.

The accounting for consideration payable to a customer is primarily concerned with making a determination of whether the payment constitutes a material right (significant and incremental) to the buyer. If the payment is deemed to be a material right that is distinct, then the seller accounts for the amount received as something other than a reduction of revenue to be recorded under the arrangement. Accounting treatment would normally be a reduction in an incurred expense, for example, the buyer reimburses the seller for advertising incurred for the buyer's products or services.

Other common forms of consideration payable to customers include:

Slotting fees—seller manufacturer pays retailer for shelf space. In this case, the manufacturer would generally record the payment as a reduction of revenue as there is no distinct benefit provided to the seller.
Up-front fees—companies may pay a fee to a customer in order to enter into a contractual agreement. These fees lack the transfer of

a distinct benefit and would generally be accounted for as a reduction of revenue.

Allocate the Transaction Price to the Separate Performance Obligations

The proposed revenue model continues use of the *relative selling price method* that was introduced in Chapter 2—Multiple-Element Arrangements. However, the new model will not incorporate the hierarchy of stand-alone value that is required to be used under current accounting guidance. The hierarchy to determine stand-alone value as the basis for allocating amounts to separate units of accounting is as follows:

Vendor-specific objective evidence (VSOE)—the price at which a product or service is sold separately.

Third-party evidence (TPE)—the price at which a similar product or service is sold by other companies.

Best estimate of selling price (BESP)—companies' estimate of what the product or service would sell for if sold separately.

The proposed model indicates that an observable market price (either VSOE or TPE) above is the preferred stand-alone value to use when allocating consideration to performance obligations. When neither VSOE nor TPE is available, companies then estimate the stand-alone value of the product or service (BESP).

Accounting guidance for determining an estimate of stand-alone selling price is as follows:[4]

If a stand-alone selling price is not directly observable, a company shall estimate it. When estimating a stand-alone selling price, the company shall consider all information (including market conditions, entity-specific factors, and information about the customer or class of customer) that is reasonably available to the entity. In addition, the company shall maximize the use of observable inputs (accounting guidance refers to observable inputs as market related) and shall apply estimation methods consistently in similar circumstances.

Suitable estimation methods include, but are not limited to, the following:

1. *Adjusted market assessment approach*—A company could evaluate the market in which it sells goods or services and estimate the price that customers in that market would be willing to pay for those goods or services. This approach also might include referring to prices from the company's competitors for similar goods or services and adjusting those prices as necessary to reflect the company's costs and margins.

2. *Expected cost plus a margin approach*—A company could forecast its expected costs of satisfying a performance obligation and then add an appropriate margin for that good or service.

3. *Residual approach*—If the stand-alone selling price of a good or service is highly variable or uncertain, then a company may estimate the stand-alone selling price by reference to the total transaction price less the sum of the observable stand-alone selling prices of other goods or services promised in the contract.

A selling price is highly variable when an entity sells the same good or service to different customers (at or near the same time) for a broad range of amounts. A selling price is uncertain when an entity has not yet established a price for a good or service and the good or service has not previously been sold.

The change from current practice is the use of the residual approach when stand-alone selling prices are highly variable. For example, Tech Company sells software, installation, and product maintenance to customers. It only sells all three deliverables packaged as one bundle. Tech could determine that the stand-alone value of the software is total contract price minus the installation and product maintenance stand-alone values.

The following illustration demonstrates the use of the residual technique.[5]

Fact Set

A consulting firm has developed a software package that it licenses to corporate customers in bundled packages with 3 years of professional consultation services. The transaction price varies significantly as a result of the consulting firm's negotiations with each new customer. The professional services offered are consistent from customer to customer, regardless of the size or complexity of the customer's business, and the selling price is always $1,000 per month when the firm sells professional services on a stand-alone basis. The firm determines that the variability in pricing in bundled arrangements is attributable only to the license.

The consulting firm enters into an arrangement with a customer for the delivery of the software license and 36 months of professional services for a total transaction price of $100,000.

Analysis

Using a residual technique to estimate the selling price of the license, the consulting firm would subtract the selling price of the professional services from the total transaction price, resulting in a selling price of $64,000 for the license ($100,000 — (36 months × $1,000)). The entity would then allocate the transaction price to each performance obligation using the relative selling price method, resulting in $64000(($64,000/$100,000) × $100,000) allocated to the license and $36,000 (($36,000/$100,000) × $100,000) allocated to the professional services.

In determining the price of options (significant discount of future purchases) embedded in revenue arrangements, the new model allows for two approaches: (a) estimating the stand-alone selling price or (b) look through the option and assume it will be exercised. This "look through" provision is not currently allowed in accounting for multiple deliverables and should make it easier for companies than estimating the stand-alone value for a discount on future purchases.

The following illustrates accounting for options in revenue arrangements.[6]

Fact Set

An aftermarket home warranty provider offers a promotion to new subscribers who pay full price for the first year of coverage that would grant them an option to renew their services for up to 2 years at a discount. The package regularly sells for $750 for 1 year of warranty services. With the promotion, the customer would be able to renew the annual warranty at the end of each year for $600. The entity concludes that this is a material right because the customer would receive a discount that is incremental to any discount available to other customers. The entity also determines that no directly observable stand-alone selling price exists for the option to renew at a discount.

Analysis A

Because the company has no directly observable evidence, the company has to estimate the stand-alone selling price of a $150 discount on the renewal of service in years 2 and 3. In coming up with this estimate, the company would likely consider factors such as the likelihood that the option will be exercised, time value of the money (as the discount is only available in future periods), and what comparable discounted offers sell for. For example, the company may consider the selling price of an offer for a discounted price of similar services found on a—deal of the day—website.

Analysis B

Rather than estimate the stand-alone selling price of the renewal option, the company chooses to allocate the transaction price by determining the consideration it expects to be entitled to in exchange for all of the services it expects to provide. Assume that the company obtained 100 new subscribers under the promotion. Based on historical experience, the company anticipates approximately 50% attrition annually, after also giving consideration to the anticipated effect that the $150 discount will have on attrition. Therefore, on the entire portfolio of new contracts, the company expects to provide warranty services for all 100 customers in the first year, 50 customers in the second year, and 25 customers in the third year. The total consideration the company expects to receive is $120,000 [(100 × $750) + (50 × $600) + (25 × $600)]. Assuming the stand-alone selling price for each warranty period is the same, the company would allocate $685.71 ($120,000/175) to each warranty period sold.

The company would recognize revenue related to the warranty services as the services are performed. During the first year, the company would recognize $68,571 (100 warranties sold × the allocated price of $685.71 per warranty). If the actual renewals in years 2 and 3 differ from expectations, the company would have to update its estimates.

The proposed model also allows an exception to allocation of the discount proportionally to the arrangement's performance obligations. When companies have arrangements that contain variable or contingent consideration, they will be required to allocate that amount to a single performance obligation if the following two conditions are met.[7]

1. The contingent payment terms for the distinct good or service relate specifically to the entity's efforts to transfer that good or service (or to a specific outcome from transferring that good or service).
2. Allocating the contingent amount of consideration entirely to the distinct good or service is consistent with the allocation principle (economics of the arrangement) when considering all of the performance obligations and payment terms in the contract.

The following examples illustrate accounting for contingent consideration.

Fact Set

An entity enters into a contract with a customer for two intellectual property licenses (License A and License B), which are two separate performance obligations. The stated price for License A is a fixed amount of $800, and for License B the price is 3% of the customer's future sales of products that use License B. The entity's estimate of the transaction price is $1,700 (which includes $900 of estimated royalties for License B). The estimated stand-alone selling prices of Licenses A and B are $800 and $1,000, respectively.

Analysis

The company would allocate the contingent royalty payment of $900 entirely to License B because that contingent payment relates specifically to an outcome from the performance obligation to transfer License B (i.e., the customer's subsequent sales of products that use License B). In addition, allocating the expected royalty amounts of $900 entirely to License B is consistent with the allocation principle in paragraph 70 when considering the other payment terms and performance obligations in the contract.

The entity transfers License B at inception of the contract and transfers License A 1 month later. Upon transfer of License B, the entity recognizes as revenue only the amount to which it is reasonably assured to be entitled. Because the expected royalty amount of $900 varies entirely on the basis of the customer's subsequent sales of products that use License B, the entity is not reasonably assured to receive that amount until the customer's subsequent sales occur.

Therefore, the entity would not recognize revenue at the $900 allocated amount until the customer sells the products that use License B. When License A is transferred, the entity would recognize as revenue the $800 allocated to License A.

Fact Set

An entity enters into a contract with a customer for two intellectual property licenses (License A and License B), which are two separate performance obligations. The stated price for License A is $300, and for License B the price is 5% of the customer's future sales of products using License B. The entity's estimate of the transaction price is $1,800 (which includes $1,500 of royalties for License B). The estimated stand-alone selling prices of Licenses A and B are $800 and $1,000, respectively.

Analysis

The company concludes that even though the contingent payment relates to subsequent sales of License B, allocating that amount entirely to License B would not be consistent with the principle for allocating the transaction price because the contingent payment does not reflect the amount to which the entity expects to be entitled in exchange for License B when considering the other payment terms and performance obligations in the contract.

The company would allocate the total transaction price of $1,800 ($300 fixed payment + $1,500 contingent payment) to Licenses A and B on a relative stand-alone selling price basis of $800 and $1,000, respectively.

The entity transfers License A at the inception of the contract and transfers License B 1 month later. Upon transfer of License A, the entity recognizes as revenue only the amount to which it is reasonably assured to be entitled. Because the $1,500 varies entirely on the basis of the customer's subsequent sales of products that use License B, the entity is not reasonably assured to receive that amount until the customer's subsequent sales occur.

Therefore, the amount of revenue recognized for License A is limited to $300 at the time of transfer of License A to the customer. Any contingent payments relating to License B would be recognized as revenue as the customer sells the products that use License B.

Satisfaction of Performance Obligations

The final phase of analysis for companies in recognizing revenue takes place when the company satisfies the promises it made to buyers and extinguishes its obligations to customers. Revenue recognition then occurs what the performance obligation the seller has contracted with the buyer to perform is satisfied. The proposed revenue model in regard to obligations being satisfied by the seller is a control model. The obligation to the buyer is extinguished (and revenue is recognized) when the customer takes control of the asset. Control is defined as "the ability of the customer to direct the use of the asset and obtain substantially all of the remaining benefits from the asset." Companies then will satisfy the requirements of the control model by transferring products and services at a point in time (completed performance) or continuous transfers over time (proportional performance).

Satisfying obligations at a point in time is analogous to the accounting guidance found in Chapter 3 on Product Revenue. The guidance in that chapter will be continued for the new revenue model. The basic concept is that when the seller transfers the risk and rewards of ownership to the buyer and the buyer has received control (access to benefits from controlling the asset), then revenue can be recognized by the seller.

When companies satisfy their performance obligations over time by delivering products and services to customers, then the process of revenue recognition can become more difficult in determining when their promises have been fulfilled. The accounting guidance for accounting for service revenue transactions is a more definitive revenue guidance, which is reliant on analogies in determining the appropriate guidance (see Chapter 2—Service Revenue).

Accounting guidance for determining a transfer of control over time is given as follows.

> An entity transfers control of a good or service over time and, hence, satisfies a performance obligation and recognizes revenue over time if at least one of the following two criteria is met:[8]
>
> 1. The entity's performance creates or enhances an asset (e.g., work in process) that the customer controls as the asset is created or enhanced. An entity shall apply the proposed guidance on control in paragraphs to determine whether the customer controls an asset as it is created or enhanced.

For example, Tech Company is installing financial management software for Services Company. The process of installing the software actively involves Services employees as the software is customized to their particular requirements. In this case, the company is controlling the asset as it is being installed. For Tech, since the software and installation are integrated for Services, it concludes that it is delivering products and services continuously and recognizes revenue as the products and services are being provided to Services.

2. The entity's performance does not create an asset with an alternative use to the entity and at least one of the following criteria is met:

(i) The customer simultaneously receives and consumes the benefits of the entity's performance as the entity performs.

For example, professional service firms performing training or consulting work would recognize revenue as the client is consuming the work. In other words, each day of training or each day of consulting is adding value for the client.

(ii) Another entity would not need to substantially re-perform the work the entity has completed to date if that other entity were to fulfill the remaining obligation to the customer. In evaluating this criterion, the entity shall presume that another entity fulfilling the remainder of the contract would not have the benefit of any asset (e.g., work in process) presently controlled by the entity. In addition, an entity shall disregard potential limitations (contractual or practical) that would prevent it from transferring a remaining performance obligation to another entity.

(iii) The entity has a right to payment for performance completed to date, and it expects to fulfill the contract as promised. The right to payment for performance completed to date does not need to be for a fixed amount. However, the entity must be entitled to an amount that is intended to at least compensate the entity for performance completed to date even if the customer can terminate the contract for reasons other than the entity's failure to perform as promised. Compensation for performance completed to date includes payment that approximates the selling price of the goods or services transferred to date (e.g., recovery of the entity's costs plus a reasonable profit margin) rather than compensation for only the entity's potential loss of profit if the contract is terminated.

Service providers who are being contractually paid based on an hourly rate would recognize the revenue as the service is being provided.

The following illustrates the accounting guidance for alternative-use assets.

Fact Set

An entity is developing residential real estate and starts marketing individual units (apartments). The entity has entered into the minimum number of contracts that are needed to begin construction.

A customer enters into a binding sales contract for a specified unit that is not yet ready for occupancy. The customer pays a nonrefundable deposit at inception of the contract and also promises to make payments throughout the contract. Those payments are intended to at least compensate the entity for performance completed to date and are refundable only if the entity fails to deliver the completed unit. The entity receives the final payment only on completion of the contract (i.e., when the customer obtains possession of the unit).

To finance the payments, the customer borrows from a financial institution that makes the payments directly to the entity on behalf of the customer. The lender has full recourse against the customer. The customer can sell his or her interest in the partially completed unit, which would require approval of the lender but not the entity. The customer is able to specify minor variations to the basic design but cannot specify or alter major structural elements of the unit's design. The contract precludes the entity from transferring the specified unit to another customer.

Analysis

The asset (apartment) created by the entity's performance does not have an alternative use to the entity because the contract has substantive terms that preclude the entity from directing the unit to another customer. The entity concludes that it has a right to payment for performance completed to date because the customer is obliged to compensate the entity for its performance rather than only a loss of profit if the contract is terminated. In addition, the entity expects to fulfill the contract as promised.

Therefore, the terms of the contract and the surrounding facts and circumstances indicate that the entity has a performance obligation that it satisfies over time. To recognize revenue for that performance obligation satisfied over time, the entity would measure its progress toward completion of the contract obligations.

When companies have determined that the performance obligation is satisfied continuously over time, accounting guidance then requires that the company select a method that most accurately depicts the transfers. The proposed revenue model has two general types of methods for companies to recognize revenue when arrangements continuously transfer products and services.

- *Output methods*: units produced, agreed-upon contract milestones, surveys of costs transferred to date compared to the total contractual amounts agreed to by the buyer and seller would be some of the more common output measures that companies could use to recognize revenue. Generally, output methods are the most representative of value being added to the buyer in depicting continuous transfers.
- *Input methods*: recognize revenue on the basis of efforts expended (materials consumed, labor hours worked, costs incurred) to date over the total expected to be delivered. The problem with these types of methods is that the incurrence of costs by the seller and the transfer of products and services may not have a direct relationship. Because a company incurs

"start-up" costs in offering products or services to customers, there is a presumption in recognizing revenue that the amounts received are not direct reimbursements for costs incurred. Revenue is "earned" when value passes to the buyer, not only when a company has incurred activities that will lead to revenue transfers from the buyer.

The following illustrates the output and input methods of revenue recognition.[9]

Fact Set

A shipbuilding entity enters into an arrangement to build its customer 15 vessels over a 3-year period. The customer played a significant role in the design of the vessels, and the entity has not built a vessel of this nature in the past. As a result, the arrangement includes both design and production services. Additionally, the entity expects that the first vessels may take longer to produce than the last vessels because, as the entity gains experience building the vessels, it expects that experience will enable it to construct the vessels more efficiently.

Analysis

Assume that the entity has determined that the design and production services represent a single performance obligation. In such situations, the entity would likely not choose a—service units of delivery method as a measure of progress because that method would not capture accurately the level of performance (as it would exclude the efforts of the entity during the design phase of the arrangement). In such situations, an entity would likely determine that an input method, such as a cost-to-cost approach, is more appropriate.

Conversely, assume that after the first 15 vessels were delivered, the customer ordered 5 additional vessels. For these vessels, the entity does not have to undertake additional design efforts. Therefore, the entity may conclude that each individual vessel represents a separate performance obligation. Alternatively, if the entity concludes that the arrangement represents a single performance obligation, the entity may determine that a—units of delivery method provides the best depiction of the continuous transfer.

When a company uses the input method to account for products and services delivered continuously, there may be instances when products are delivered and the customer obtains control, but the services related to those products have not been performed. For example, contractors often have materials delivered to the construction site, prior to those materials being installed. In this case, accounting guidance for companies use the input approach that would record revenue at an amount equal to the cost of the product.

The following illustrates the accounting guidance for this situation.

Fact Set

An entity enters into a contract with a customer to construct a facility for $140 million over 2 years. The contract also requires the entity to procure specialized equipment from a third party and integrate that equipment into the facility. The entity expects to transfer control of the specialized equipment approximately 6 months from when the project begins. The installation and integration of the equipment continue throughout the contract. The contract is a single performance obligation because all of the promised goods or services in the contract are highly inter-related and the entity also provides a significant service of integrating those goods or services into the single facility for which the customer has contracted. In addition, the entity significantly modifies the bundle of goods and services to fulfill the contract. The entity measures progress toward complete satisfaction of the performance obligation on the basis of costs incurred relative to total costs expected to be incurred.

At contract inception, the entity expects the following:

Transaction price :	$140,000,000
Cost of the specialized equipment:	$40,000,000
Other costs:	$80,000,000
Total expected costs:	$120,000,000

The company concludes that the best depiction of the entity's performance is to recognize revenue for the specialized equipment in an amount equal to the cost of the specialized equipment upon the transfer of control to the customer. Hence, the entity would exclude the cost of the specialized equipment from its measure of progress toward complete satisfaction of the performance obligation on a cost-to-cost basis and account for the contract as follows.

During the first 6 months, the entity incurs $20,000,000 of costs relative to the total $80,000,000 of expected costs (excluding the $40,000,000 cost of the specialized equipment). Hence, the entity estimates that the performance obligation is 25% complete ($20,000,000 ÷ $80,000,000) and recognizes a revenue of $25,000,000 (25% × $140,000,000 total transaction price − $40,000,000 revenue for the specialized equipment).

Upon transfer of control of the specialized equipment, the entity recognizes revenue and costs of $40,000,000. Subsequently, the entity continues to recognize revenue on the basis of costs incurred relative to total expected costs (excluding the revenue and cost of the specialized equipment).

Accounting for Contract Costs

In an expansion of current accounting practice, companies will be allowed to record an asset (deferred cost) for contract fulfillment costs for revenue arrangements. The company will then amortize (write-off) the deferred costs against the expected revenue stream as performance obligations are performed. Costs that will qualify for recording as an asset will be the direct and incremental costs in fulfilling contractual terms. This accounting treatment will provide, for companies that choose this option, a better matching of incurred costs against the revenue streams to be received in determining profitability of customer revenue arrangements.

The costs eligible for asset treatment (capitalized costs) will be required to meet all of the following criteria.[10]

1. The costs relate *directly* to the contract.
2. The costs generate or enhance the resources of the company that will be used in satisfying performance obligation in the future. (Costs incurred that build productive capacity in fulfilling customer obligations relating to revenue arrangements.)
3. The costs are expected to be recovered through payments received in revenue arrangements with customers.

Costs that relate directly to the contract, which are eligible to be capitalized and amortized over the revenue arrangement include:

• Salaries and wages of employees who provide services directly to the customer.
• Direct materials used in providing services to the customer.
• Allocations of costs that relate directly to producing the contract or for contract activities. Those would primarily be infrastructure costs incurred for building productive capacity such as contract management and administrative costs, insurance, and depreciation of equipment used in fulfilling the contract. When making this allocation the cost to the revenue arrangement, it is important that the cost be directly incurred in fulfilling contractual obligations.
• Costs that are chargeable to customers as specified under the terms and conditions of the contractual.

Incremental costs of fulfilling a contract are defined as "those costs that a company incurs in its efforts to obtain a contract with a customer and that it would not have incurred if the contract had not been obtained" (ED #95). When companies incur costs that would have been incurred whether or not the contract was obtained, companies shall expense those costs as incurred. For example, you have a salesperson who is compensated by salary and commission. The salesperson is successful in getting customer to sign a 4-year contract in which company will deliver consulting services for a fee of $4,000,000. The commission is 5%; so the salesperson gets $200,000 on contract signing. The commission is allowed to be capitalized as a deferred cost and amortized over the 4-year revenue stream. The salesperson's salary would be expensed when incurred.

Amortization (write-off of the asset) shall be on a systematic and rational basis that corresponds to the pattern of transfers of products and services. In addition, the entity will update the asset account for any changes in the pattern of transfer of promised products and services.

The following illustrates the accounting for contract fulfillment costs.

Fact Set

An entity enters into a contract to outsource a customer's information technology data center for 5 years. The entity incurs selling commission costs of $10,000 to obtain the contract. Before providing the services, the entity designs and builds a technology platform that interfaces with the customer's systems. That platform is not transferred to the customer. The customer promises to pay a fixed fee of $20,000 per month.

Analysis

The $10,000 incremental costs of obtaining the contract are recognized as an asset. The asset is amortized over the term of the contract. The initial costs incurred to set up the technology platform are as follows:

Design services: $40,000
Hardware: $120,000
Software: $90,000
Migration and testing of datacenter: $10,000

The initial setup costs relate primarily to activities to fulfill the contract but do not transfer goods or services to the customer.

The entity would account for the initial setup costs as follows:

1. Hardware costs—accounted for as the asset equipment and depreciated over its expected useful life

2. Software costs—accounted for as an asset, if proprietary to the firm, and amortized over their expected useful life

3. Costs of the design, migration, and testing of the datacenter—considered for capitalization as an contract fulfillment asset and amortized over the 5-year contractual term as outsourced services are provided to the customer

The following illustrates accounting for amortization of capitalized contract fulfillment costs.

Fact Set

An entity enters into a contract with a customer for 1 year of transaction-processing services. The entity charges the customer a nonrefundable up-front fee in part as compensation for the initial activities of setting up the customer on the entity's systems and processes. The customer can renew the contract each year without paying the initial fee.

Analysis

The entity's setup activities do not transfer any service to the customer and, hence, do not give rise to a performance obligation. Therefore, the entity recognizes as revenue the initial fee over the period that it expects to provide services to the customer, which may exceed the 1 year of the initial contract term.

The incurred setup costs enhance resources of the entity that will be used in satisfying performance obligations in the future, and those costs are expected to be recovered. Therefore, the entity would recognize the setup costs as an asset, which would be amortized over the period that the entity expects to provide services to the customer (consistent with the pattern of revenue recognition), which may exceed the 1 year of the initial contract term.

The proposed standard on revenue recognition is predicted to be completed by the second quarter of 2013, with application no earlier than

2016. The IASB and the FASB, however, continue to make changes to the proposed standard; so this chapter is current as of December 31, 2012. The impact on accounting for revenue transactions is far reaching as there will be a single model for almost all industries to use in applying the realization and recognition concepts in recording revenue in financial statements. The chapters on multiple-element arrangements and product and service revenue recognition will be very helpful in applying the new standard.

This completes Revenue Recognition: Principles and Practices. My intent was to provide a useable book that clearly and concisely describes accounting for revenue accounting for multiple deliverable arrangements, product arrangements, and service arrangements. This chapter is designed as a stand-alone treatment of the new revenue model proposed by the accounting standard setters. As you apply the principles and practices for revenue arrangements, please keep in mind that companies need to exercise professional judgment in applying the accounting guidance and to apply that guidance consistently across financial reporting periods.

Notes

Chapter 1

1. Financial Accounting Standards Board (FASB); Concept Statement No. 5, Recognition and Measurement in Financial Statements of Business Enterprises.
2. www.sec.gov. Topic 13: Revenue in Financial Statements.
3. FASB Accounting Standards Codification (ASC) 605-10-S99, A2, ques. 1.
4. FASB ASC 605-15-05-3.
5. There are numerous examples to be found in SEC Topic 13: Revenue in Financial Statements
6. Accounting Standards Codification (ASC) 605-15-25

Chapter 2

1. FASB ASC 985-605-15-3(d).
2. FASB ASC 605-25-25-5.
3. FASB ASC 605-25-25-5.
4. FASB ASC 605-20.
5. FASB ASC 605-10-S99, C.
6. FASB ASC 605-10-S99, ques. 2.
7. FASB ASC 605-25-30-6a, 6b, 6c.
8. FASB ASC 605-25-25-30 and FASB ASC 605-25-25-55-37.

Chapter 3

1. FASB ASC 605-10-S99, A2, ques. 2.
2. FASB ASC 605-10-S99-A2.
3. FASB ASC 470-15-2.
4. Taub (2013).
5. FASB ASC 605-15-25.
6. FASB ASC 605-10-S99, A3b, ques. 1.
7. FASB ASC 605-10-S99, A3b, ques. 3, 4, 5.
8. FASB ASC 605-50-25-3.
9. FASB ASC 605-50-25-4.
10. FASB ASC 605-55-80.

11. FASB ASC 605-50-25-7.
12. FASB ASC 605-45-45.
13. FASB ASC 605-45-45-55,56.

Chapter 4

1. Taub (2013).
2. FASB ASC 605-10-S99, A4d.
3. Taub (2013).
4. FASB 605-10-S99, A3f, ques. 1, 2.
5. Taub (2013).
6. FASB ASC 605-15-25.
7. FASB ASC 405-20-40.

Chapter 5

1. Accounting Standards Update (ASU), paragraph 14.
2. ASU, paragraph 29.
3. ASU, paragraph 52.
4. ASU, paragraph 73.
5. Ernst & Young (2011).
6. Ernst & Young (2011).
7. ASU, paragraph 76.
8. ASU, paragraph 35–37.
9. Ernst & Young (2011).
10. ASU, paragraph 91.

References

Ernst & Young. (2011). Technical line. *Double exposure: The revised revenue recognition proposal.* From www.ey.com/us/accountinglink

Financial Accounting Standards Board (FASB). (2010). *Accounting Standards Codification (ASC)* TM .

Financial Accounting Standards Board (FASB). (November 14, 2011). *Proposed Accounting Standards Update (ASU).* Revenue Recognition (Topic 605). Revenue from Contracts with Customers.

Taub, Scott. (2013). *Revenue Recognition Guide*, CCH 2013 Edition .

Index

N
Net revenue, 72

O
Outsourcing contract costs, 94–95
Ownership risks and rewards, 47–48

P
Performance model
  Completed Performance model
    completed services, 77
    financial planner, 77–78
    space lease broker, 79–80
  health-care providers, 80
  Proportional Performance model,
    77–78
    accounting company audit,
      82–84
    American Airlines Corporation
      10-K, 84
    discrete activities, 82
    dissimilar activities, 82
    payment-processing firm, 82
    relative-selling-price
      method, 82
    service transaction, 80
    similar/nonsimilar activities, 81
    Six Flags Entertainment
      Corporation 10-K, 84
    value-creating activities, 80–81
  seller activities, 78–79
  service deliverable, 78
Performance obligations
  identification
    Completed Performance model,
      111
    customer relationship
      management software,
      112–113
    outfitting office space, 115–116
    Proportional Performance model,
      111–112
    specialty construction firm,
      113–114
    volume discount, 116–117
  satisfaction
    accounting guidance, 135–136
    alternative-use assets, 132–134
    control model, 130

output and input methods,
  134–135
professional service firms,
  131–132
revenue model, 129–130
transfer control, 130–131
Persuasive evidence, 47
  accounting issues, 6–7
  contractual arrangement, 5
  EDI, 6
  enforceable claims, 5
  formal sales contract, 5–6
  OPNET Technologies, Inc. Form
    10-K, 7
Product financing arrangements,
  51–53
Product revenue
  Completed Performance model, 47
  customer acceptance provisions
    customer-specified performance
      criteria, 59
    IBM 10-K, 60–61
    revenue issues, 59–60
    sales transaction cancellation, 58
    seller-specified criteria, 58–59
  customer return rights
    accounting criteria, 53–54
    example illustration, 55
    exchange rights, 53
    P&L statement, 53
    returns amount estimation, 54
    sales patterns and trends, 55
  future purchases discounts, 65–66
  gift cards
    Apple Corporation 10-K, 68–69
    Chipotle 10K, 69–70
    usage prediction, 68
  gross vs. net revenue reporting
    Apple Corporation 10-K, 73–75
    FedEx 10-K, 75–76
    gross revenue, 70–72
    net revenue, 72
  involvement after delivery
    Advanced Micro Devices, Inc.,
      10-K, 49–51
    "in-substance" consignment, 49
    qualitative guidance, 49
  ownership risks and rewards, 47–48
  point and loyalty programs, 66–68

OTHER TITLES IN FINANCIAL ACCOUNTING AND AUDITING COLLECTION

Scott Showalter, NC State University and Jan Williams, University of Tennessee, Collection Editors

- *An Executive's Guide for Moving from US GAAP to IFRS* by Peter Walton
- *Effective Financial Management: The Cornerstone for Success* by Geoff Turner
- *Financial Reporting Standards: A Decision-Making Perspective for Non-Accountants* by David Doran

ALSO, FROM OUR MANAGERIAL ACCOUNTING COLLECTION

Kenneth A. Merchant, University of Southern California, Collection Editor

- *Business Planning and Entrepreneurship: An Accounting Approach* by Michael Kraten
- *Corporate Investment Decisions: Principles and Practice* by Michael Pogue
- *Revenue Management: A Path to Increased Profits* by Ronald Huefner
- *Cost Management and Control in Government Fighting the Cost War Through Leadership Driven Management* by Dale Geiger
- *Drivers of Successful Controllership: Activities, People, and Connecting with Management* by Jurgen Weber and Pascal Nevries
- *Setting Performance Targets* by Carolyn Stringer and Paul Shantapriyan
- *Strategic Cost Analysis* by Roger Hussey and Audra Ong

Announcing the Business Expert Press Digital Library

Concise E-books Business Students Need for Classroom and Research

This book can also be purchased in an e-book collection by your library as
- a one-time purchase,
- that is owned forever,
- allows for simultaneous readers,
- has no restrictions on printing, and
- can be downloaded as PDFs from within the library community.

Our digital library collections are a great solution to beat the rising cost of textbooks. e-books can be loaded into their course management systems or onto student's e-book readers.

The **Business Expert Press** digital libraries are very affordable, with no obligation to buy in future years. For more information, please visit **www.businessexpertpress.com/librarians**. To set up a trial in the United States, please contact **Adam Chesler** at *adam.chesler@businessexpertpress.com* for all other regions, contact **Nicole Lee** at *nicole.lee@igroupnet.com*.